Plains Indian Museum

Curator's Notes

Edited by Emma I. Hansen

Authors

Emma I. Hansen

Rebecca T. Menlove

Anne Marie Shriver

Rebecca S. West

Plains Indian Museum

Buffalo Bill Historical Center

Cody, Wyoming

Plains Indian Museum Curator's Notes

Copy Editing and Production
Joan T. Anderson
Kimber Swenson
Rights and Reproductions
Ann Marie Donoghue

Designed by West Office Exhibition Design
Oakland, California

Buffalo Bill Historical Center
720 Sheridan Avenue
Cody, Wyoming 82414
1.307.587.4771

www.bbhc.org

ISBN 0-931618-59-2

Second Printing 2005
Sung In Printing, Korea

To purchase this book call
1.800.533.3838

Cover and Chapter Image: Shield and Cover, Northern Plains, ca. 1860. Rawhide, tanned deer hide, pigments, glass beads, wool, feathers. 21.5 in. x 2.25 in. Chandler-Pohrt Collection. Gift of Mr. and Mrs. Edson W. Spencer. NA. 108.105

Contents

Introduction

Emma I. Hansen
Curator of the Plains Indian Museum

The Great Plains region stretches from the foothills of the Rocky Mountains in the West to the Mississippi River in the East and from Canada to Texas. The Native people of the Plains found this vast, harsh, land to be rich in resources, with tall grass prairies abundant with herds of buffalo and other grazing animals and fertile river valleys that supported farming traditions. Known by the tribal names of Arapaho, Cheyenne, Blackfeet, Lakota, Shoshone, Pawnee, Gros Ventre, Assiniboine, Mandan, Hidatsa, Arikara, Kiowa, and Comanche, among others, they once dominated this region.

In American popular culture, 19th century Plains buffalo hunters often symbolize all Native Americans with the resultant view of contemporary tribal members as remnants of a nostalgic past. Plains Indian people today, however, are not frozen in the past but live as vital members of their own communities. They revere the lives of elders and those who came before them. They respect and celebrate their own diverse tribal heritages and traditions, but they also innovate and create their own futures on reservations and in small towns and cities.

Through exhibitions, publications, and educational programs, the Plains Indian Museum of the Buffalo Bill Historical Center tells the stories of Plains Native people as they have moved from their buffalo hunting past to the living traditions of the present. Established officially in 1969, the Plains Indian Museum opened as a separate wing of the Buffalo Bill Historical Center in 1979. The design and philosophy of the Museum were developed under the guidance and assistance of a Plains Indian Museum Advisory Board, consisting of artists, historians, educators, and traditional leaders from Northern Plains tribes.

In 1999, the Museum was closed while entirely new exhibitions were installed to create, in the words of Advisory Board member Joe Medicine Crow, "a living breathing place where more than just Indian objects are on display." The newly reinterpreted Plains Indian Museum opened in June 2000. The new exhibition galleries, products of five years of planning, provide the cultural contexts for the Museum's internationally significant collections. The Museum now tells the stories of Plains Indian people — their cultural backgrounds, traditions, values, and histories as well as the contexts of their lives today.

The concept and design for *Curator's Notes* were developed in the process of planning the new Museum exhibitions in partnership with West Office Exhibition Design. Over the years that I have been curator of the Plains Indian Museum, visitors have often asked questions about the materials, origins of tribal designs, artistic techniques, and other specifics pertaining to the objects exhibited in the Museum. Limited space within exhibition cases makes it difficult to answer those detailed questions. However, notebooks of *Curator's Notes* placed in front of cases in the newly installed galleries provide a means to highlight those details and address commonly asked questions about Plains Indian art and cultures.

All of the Plains Indian Museum *Curator's Notes* have been assembled in this notebook in answer to requests from educators, Museum volunteers, and Museum visitors. We have also added a page at the end of each chapter for Museum visitors to make their own notes about the superb examples of Native American art on exhibit as they explore the Plains Indian Museum.

Curator's Notes
Migration

Seasonal Mobility

Through seasonal migrations, tribes were able to both use and sustain the varied natural resources of the Plains. Nomadic buffalo hunters moved often, according to the availability of game, water, and wild plants. Even tribes that farmed in riverside villages left to hunt on the prairies after planting and harvesting. Trade and tribal wars also contributed to tribal movements.

Gros Ventre Parfleche Case

This flat container, only about three inches thick, was used to store clothing or food.

Parfleche designs were painted with reed brushes or buffalo bones.

The design was sometimes outlined, then filled in. Early examples of parfleche containers had designs cut into them.

Yellow is from crushed daffodils, other yellow flowers, or yellow ochre.

Traders introduced dried pigments in greens and dark blues.

Case is closed and secured with leather ties, then attached to a saddle.

Crow Cylinder Case

A cylinder case was used to store a feather bonnet.

The bonnet slides into the case when rolled-up, keeping feathers clean and intact.

The shape of the container adapted to its contents.

Feather bonnets were rolled for storage.

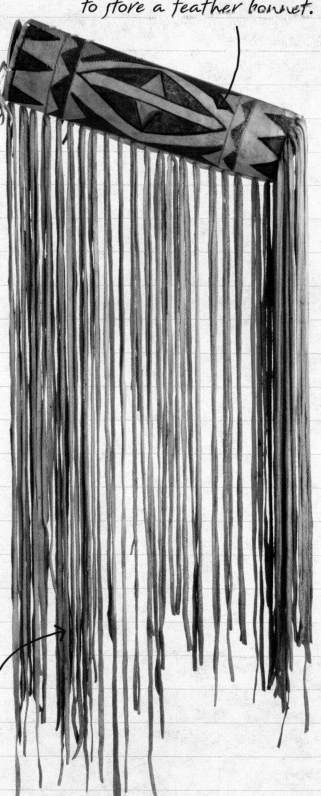

Case is sometimes attached to a saddle for adornment; note the extra-long decorative fringe.

Climate of the Plains

Many climatic factors influenced, and continue to influence, the people, animals, and natural resources of the Plains, making it a difficult and dangerous place to live.

The Land of the Atsina
Photo by Edward S. Curtis, 1908

Average recorded yearly rainfall in the last 30 years is 12-16 inches, borderline amounts for crops grown without irrigation.

Temperatures in the Plains average 10°F in winter, 80°F in summer.

Some Plains states like Wyoming, Montana, and Colorado have mountains above 6,000 feet, where it can snow almost any month of the year.

Other climatic factors include frequent high winds, tornados, hailstorms, low humidity, severe thunderstorms, flash floods, droughts, blizzards, and unexpected frosts.

The Wood Gatherer—Lakota
Photo by Edward S. Curtis, 1908

Shoshone Winter Moccasins

Unadorned winter moccasins with hide, fur, and parfleche sole from a buffalo.

Fur side in for warmth

Flap for keeping out snow

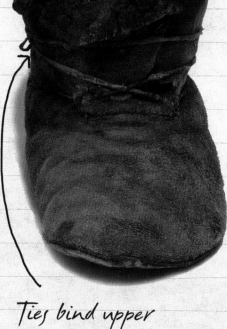

Hard parfleche sole, sewn onto bottom as a separate piece, was more durable for travel over ice and snow.

Ties bind upper part of moccasin around ankle

Blackfeet Capote

A capote (a French word for cape or cloak) was worn by French trappers/traders, and its use spread to other traders and Indian tribes.

Often made from a wool blanket or blanket material, the capote is an excellent winter garment that is warm, stops wind and sheds some water.

Stripes on the blanket indicate the weight or value of the cloth.

This type of blanket, called a "Hudson's Bay Blanket," was produced by Hudson Bay Trading Company and is still made today.

Crow Bowcase and Quiver

Essential gear for a warrior and hunter

Quiver section for arrows

Bow in here

Shoulder strap

Painted parfleche design

As firearms replaced bows and arrows, beaded and painted gun cases appeared.

The two containers, attached and carried as one unit, are slung over the shoulder for easy access on horseback.

Respecting Resources

Plains cultures do not regard the earth, elements, and animals as resources to be used up.

Photo by Ken Blackbird

Ceremonies show respect and thanks, and promise future availability of the resource.

Ceremonies honor animal or plant spirits after hunts, and after planting and harvesting. They vary depending on the lifestyles of the tribes; for example, since they were a horticultural tribe, the Chahiksichahiks (Pawnee) hold a major ceremony to thank Mother Corn.

Every object, even this plain and well-worn bag, has a story behind it. A buffalo-calling ceremony, followed by the hunt and a thanking ceremony, preceded the creation of the bag.

Crow storage bag

On the move... reasons for migration

Piegan Lodge
Photo by Edward S. Curtis, 1910

Lakota trunk, ca. 1890

Historically, Plains tribes moved periodically—several times a year, or once a year depending on lifestyle—for the following reasons:

- Follow buffalo or other game
- Move stock or horses to wintering ground
- Sanitary reasons—to keep the camp clean and allow soil and vegetation to recover
- Availability of firewood
- Availability of water year-round
- Important events, such as traveling to a Sun Dance or other major ceremonies, planting or harvesting crops, or attending talks or negotiations
- Changing trade routes/posts

Notes

Curator's Notes

Horses

Mobility on the Plains

When horses were introduced to the Plains in the 17th century, they were quickly integrated into nearly every aspect of Plains Indian life. Horses increased the distance that bands could travel and the quantity of goods they could carry, and enabled them to hunt and wage war more successfully. As horses became crucial to Plains life, they became important sources of wealth and prestige.

Plains Indian Museum

Upper Missouri River Saddle Blanket

Early example of Northern Plains saddle blanket, ca. 1835

Plains horse gear incorporated distinctive designs, combining hides and other natural materials with trade items such as glass beads, metals, and cloth.

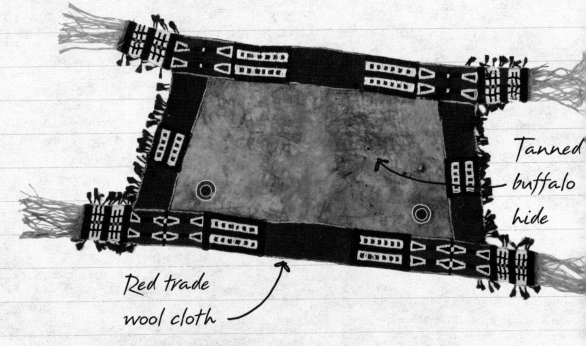

Tanned buffalo hide

Red trade wool cloth

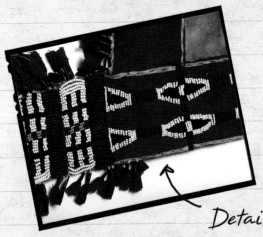

As horses were dispersed throughout the Northern Plains, tribes developed new equipment, some based upon Euro-American models.

Detail of beaded border design

Cree Pad Saddle

For hunting and warfare, pad saddles and stirrups helped to steady riders while they were shooting bows and firearms.

Wool cloth

Tanned deer hide stuffed with animal hair

Metal loops for cinch straps

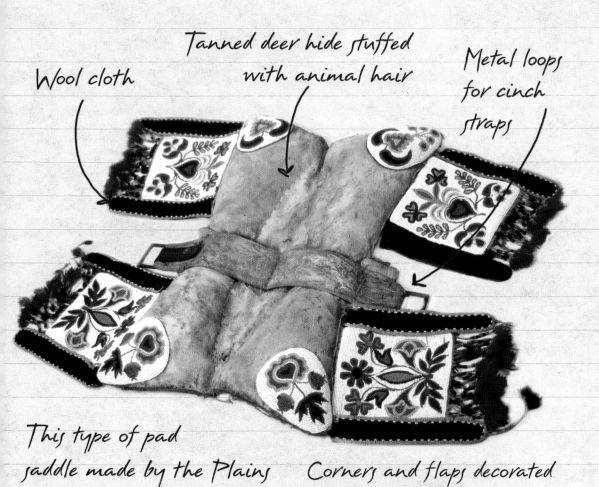

This type of pad saddle made by the Plains Cree sometimes was traded to the Blackfoot and Dakota.

Corners and flaps decorated with floral beadwork

Both men and women used beaded pad saddles for reservation parades and other special events.

Crow Girl's Saddle

Crow women's saddles with decorated stirrups, saddle blankets, horse collars, cruppers, and bridles were used for parades and other dress occasions.

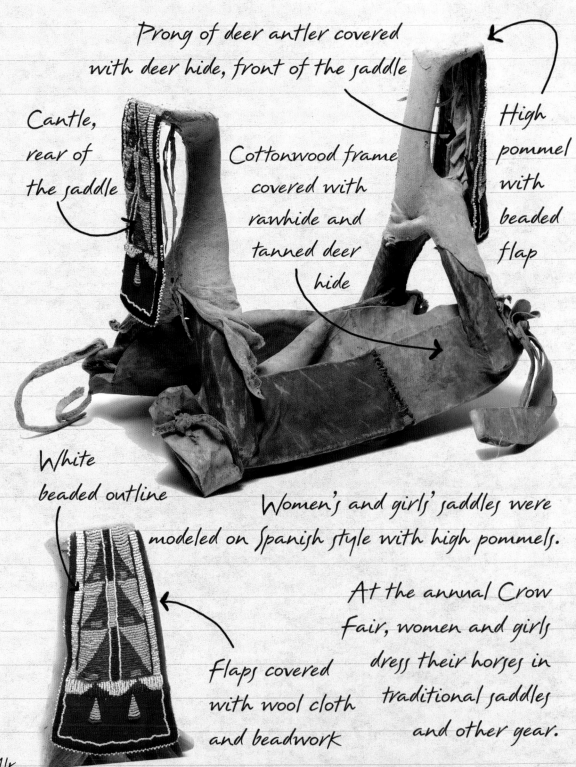

Prong of deer antler covered with deer hide, front of the saddle

Cantle, rear of the saddle

Cottonwood frame covered with rawhide and tanned deer hide

High pommel with beaded flap

White beaded outline

Women's and girls' saddles were modeled on Spanish style with high pommels.

At the annual Crow Fair, women and girls dress their horses in traditional saddles and other gear.

Flaps covered with wool cloth and beadwork

Crow Bridle

Example of adaptation of Spanish horse equipment with added tribal embellishments

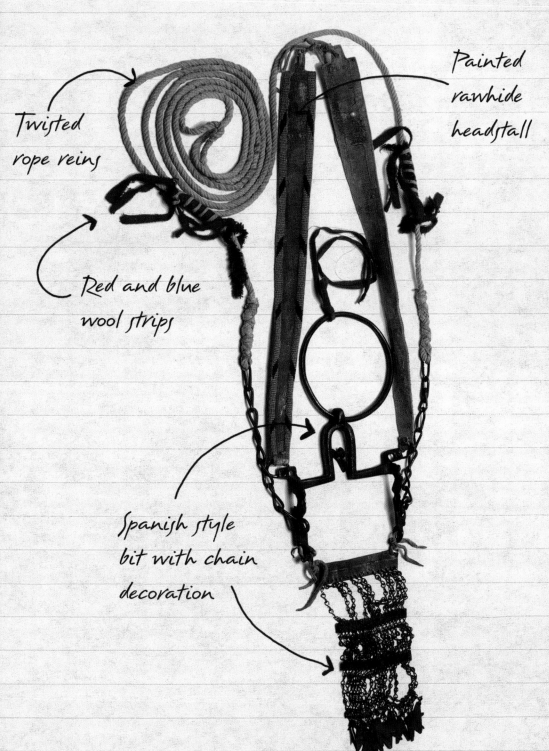

Twisted rope reins

Painted rawhide headstall

Red and blue wool strips

Spanish style bit with chain decoration

Crow Crupper

Decorated crupper is part of a parade outfit.

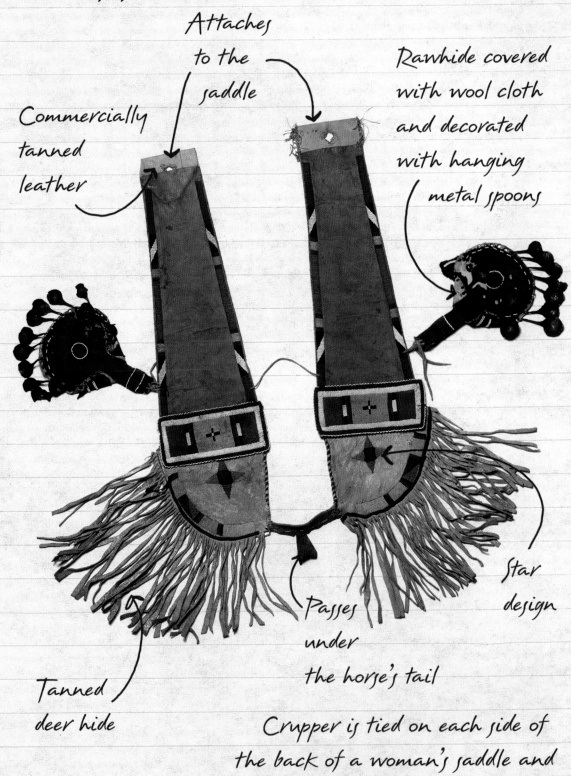

Attaches to the saddle

Rawhide covered with wool cloth and decorated with hanging metal spoons

Commercially tanned leather

Tanned deer hide

Passes under the horse's tail

Star design

Crupper is tied on each side of the back of a woman's saddle and passed under the horse's tail.

Crow Saddlebags

Older example of saddlebags decorated with wool trade cloth and glass pony and seed beads

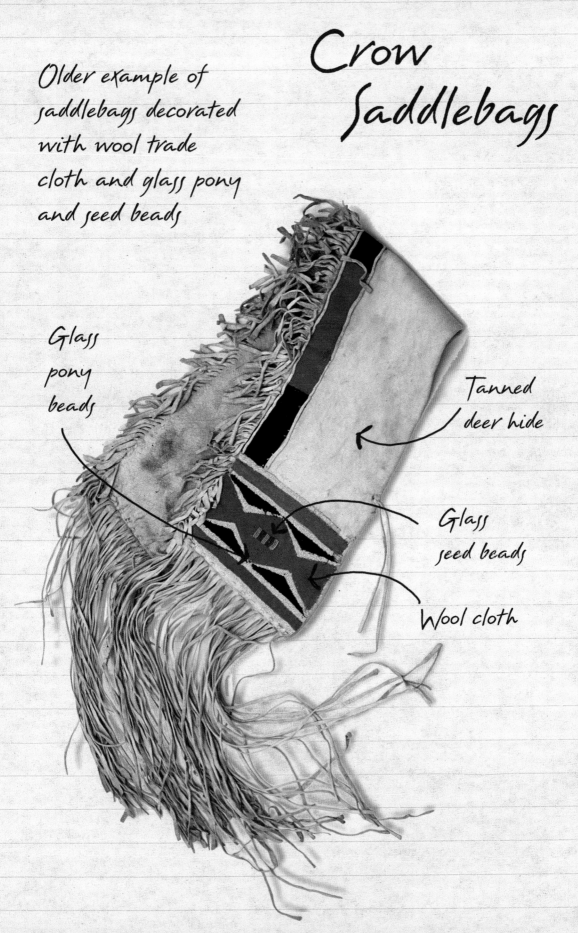

Glass pony beads

Tanned deer hide

Glass seed beads

Wool cloth

Lakota Saddlebags

Saddlebags with pockets on each side to carry belongings were thrown over horses' backs.

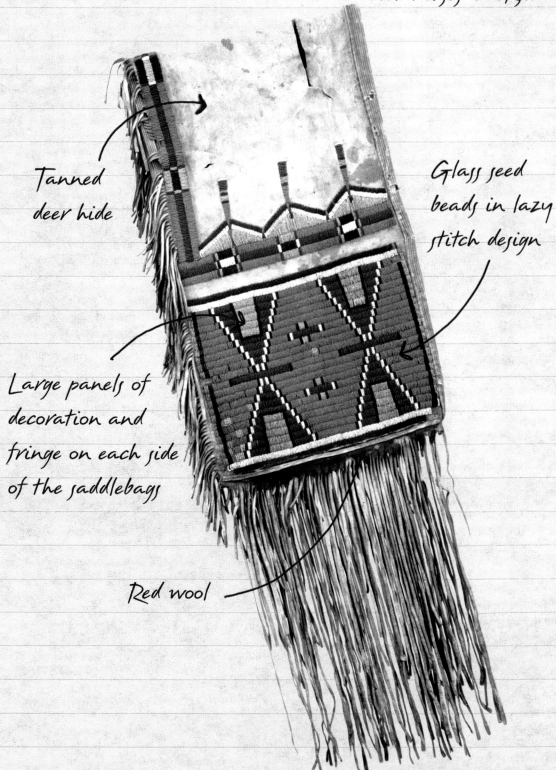

Tanned deer hide

Glass seed beads in lazy stitch design

Large panels of decoration and fringe on each side of the saddlebags

Red wool

Lakota Bag & Pipe Bowl & Stem

The significance of the horse in Plains cultures is reflected in the decorated horse equipment created for its use, as well as depictions in art—carved, painted and beaded cultural materials.

Beaded figure of a horse

Tanned deer hide

Floral design on other side

Carved horse figure on bowl

Pipe stem with floral design

Notes

Curator's Notes
Trade

Patterns of Exchange

Since ancient times, Indian people have traded with neighboring tribes and distant groups alike. Plains Indians, located at the center of vast coast-to-coast networks, have mediated between cultural groups exchanging raw materials, traditional arts, and food surpluses. Trade relationships were often cemented through adoption or marriage, resulting in influential and broadly dispersed alliances. By the time Europeans arrived on the Plains, their glass beads, colored cloth, iron implements, and guns had preceded them along well-established and dynamic Native trade routes.

Plains Indian Museum

Hairpipe Necklace

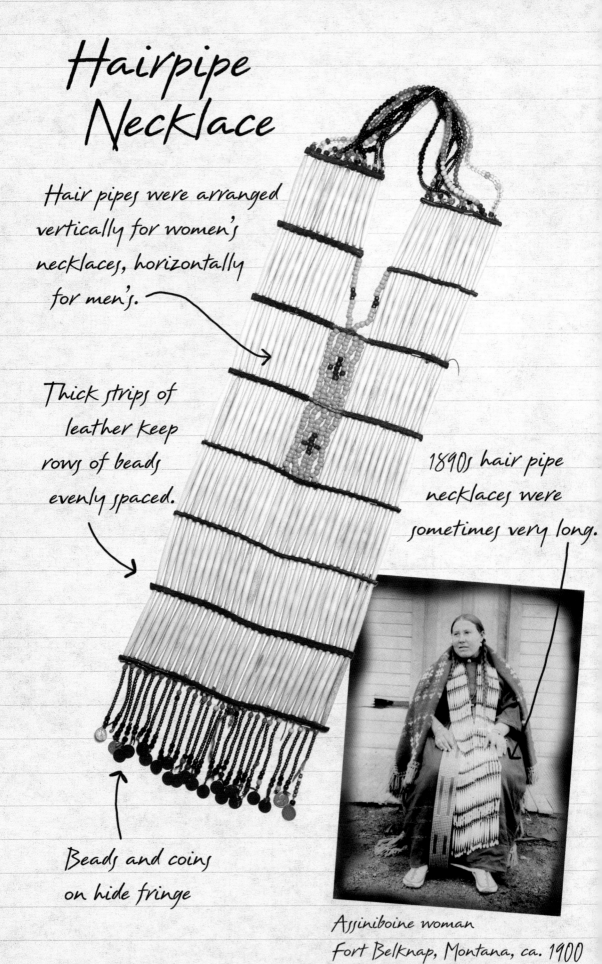

Hair pipes were arranged vertically for women's necklaces, horizontally for men's.

Thick strips of leather keep rows of beads evenly spaced.

1890s hair pipe necklaces were sometimes very long.

Beads and coins on hide fringe

Assiniboine woman
Fort Belknap, Montana, ca. 1900

Upper Missouri Leggings

"Pony" beads arrived by pony pack trains in the early 1800s; simple, bold designs make good use of their large size and limited palette.

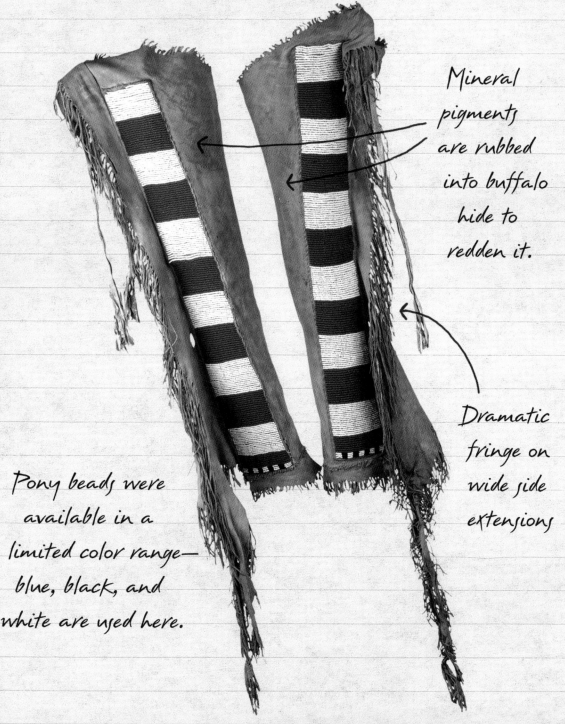

Mineral pigments are rubbed into buffalo hide to redden it.

Dramatic fringe on wide side extensions

Pony beads were available in a limited color range— blue, black, and white are used here.

Arikara Rattle

Dew claws, which make a soft, rain-like sound, are incised, split, and used intact.

A large brass bell adds a secondary sound.

Mineral pigments have worn away from handling.

Deer hide is rubbed with yellow ochre and twisted into fringe.

Bullet casings

Lakota Rifle Case

An increase in brilliantly dyed colors occurred with the expanded trade in dyes.

Porcupine quills are embroidered on hide panels, then stitched to a canvas case.

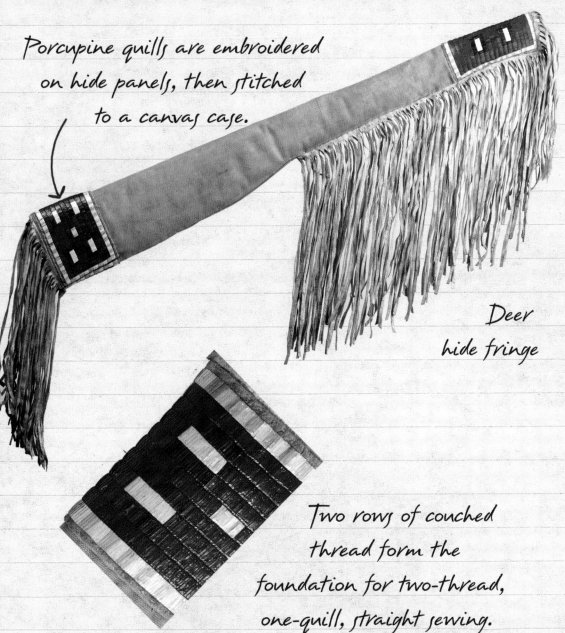

Deer hide fringe

Two rows of couched thread form the foundation for two-thread, one-quill, straight sewing.

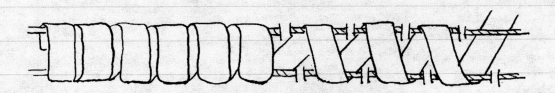

25

Lakota Knife & Case

Useful tools from Euro-American sources were widely traded among tribes; direct contact with White traders was not necessary to obtain such material.

Beadwork knife case made to personalize and preserve a trade knife.

Tin cones for embellishment. Like glass beads, the source is via trade, but the application is clearly a Native innovation.

Beads stitched along edge

Iron implements were traded along with hides and quill work, simply new additions to lively inter-tribal trade.

Four Point Hudson's Bay Blanket

Trade blanket from the Hudson's Bay Company, a key item during the height of the beaver fur trade

"Points" woven into trade blankets indicate the number of pelts required to trade for the blanket.

All-wool blankets made great winter wraps and were also sewn into coats, known as capotes.

Photographer Roland Reed captures a return to camp— a Blackfeet man carries a trade blanket over his arm.

Blackfeet camp, Montana, ca. 1910

Bone hair pipes

Shells & Beads

Elk teeth

Metal beads

Cowrie shell

Polychrome glass beads

Seed beads

Pony beads

Abalone

Wound beads (glass)

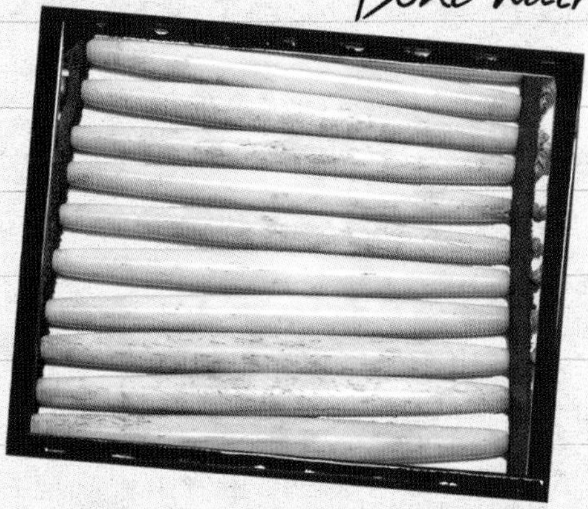

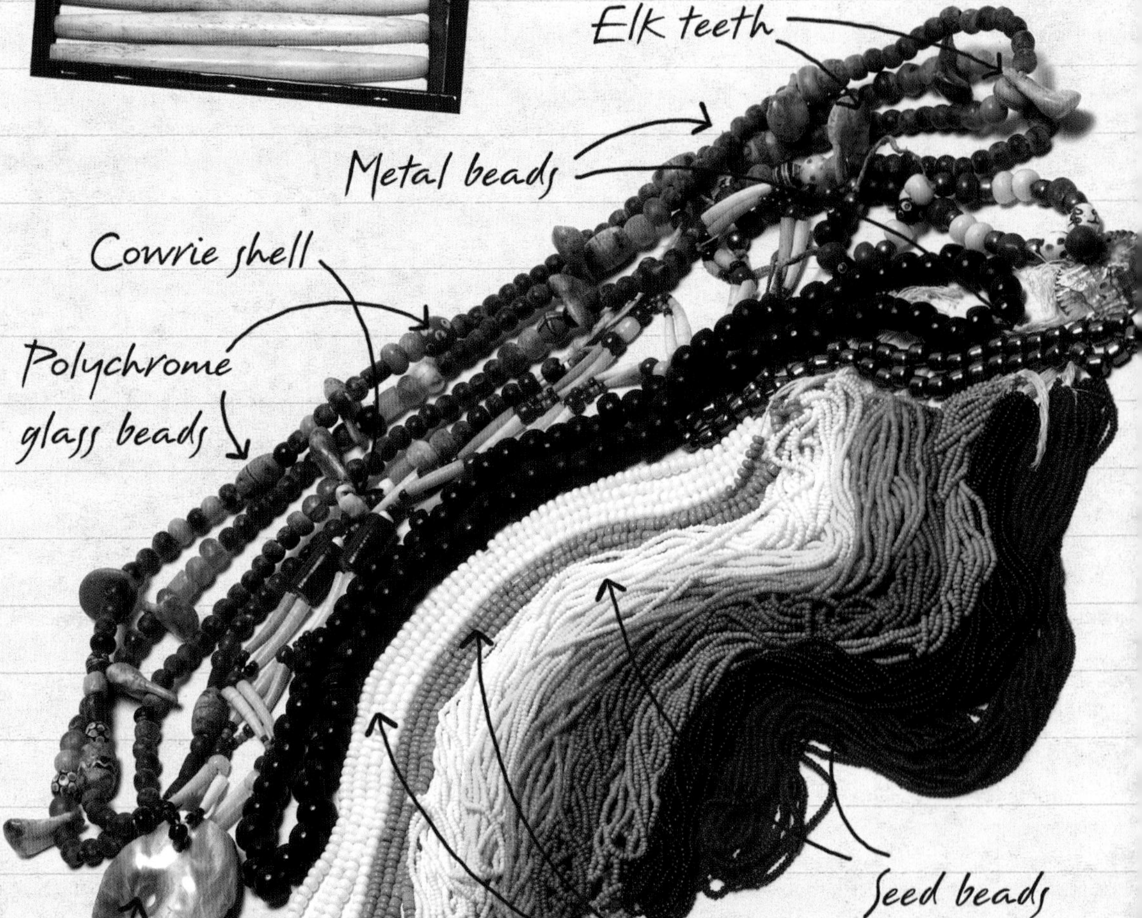

Dentalium

Trade Map

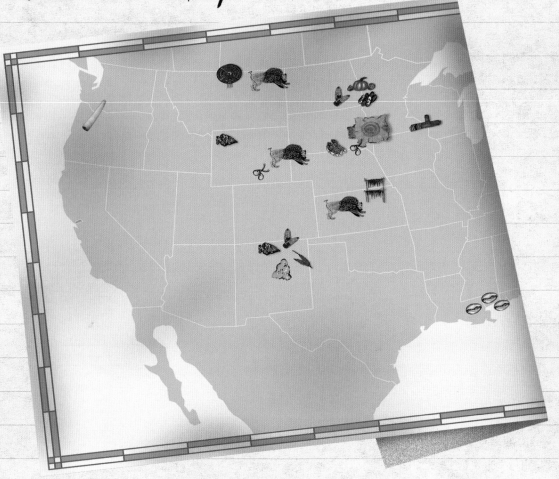

Trade Goods

 Buffalo hides

 Turquoise

 Quillwork

 Cowrie shells

 Obsidian

 Pipestone

 Worked hide goods (moccasins)

 Dentalium

 Meat

 Feathers

 Elk teeth

 Corn

 Buffalo

 Beans

 Pumpkins & squash

Notes

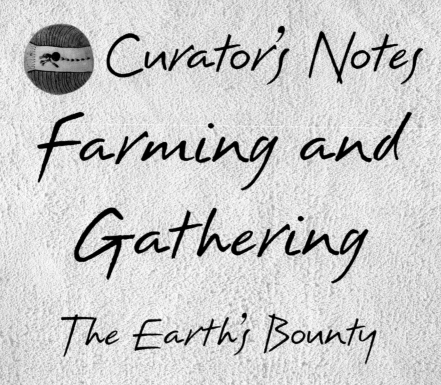

Curator's Notes

Farming and Gathering

The Earth's Bounty

The women of the Mandan, Hidatsa, and Arikara tribes contributed both to their families' diets and to the trade economy from the bounty of their gardens. In the fertile flood-plains of the Upper Missouri river, they grew squash, beans, sunflowers, and corn in gardens measuring up to three and a half acres. They also gathered wild turnips, berries, and various types of roots.

Plains Indian Museum

The Gardens at Like-a-Fishhook Village

Buffalo Bird Woman's family garden, at its largest, was 3 1/2 acres.

Map of Gardens S.E. of village.

A smallpox epidemic in 1837-1838 devastated the Mandan and Hidatsa people of Five Villages on the Upper Missouri River. The remaining few hundred Mandan and Hidatsa united in 1845 and moved to Like-a-Fishhook Village, where they continued their farming traditions. They were joined by the Arikara in 1862.

A drawing of the gardens lying southeast of
Like-a-Fishhook Village, as described by Buffalo
Bird Woman to anthropologist Gilbert Wilson

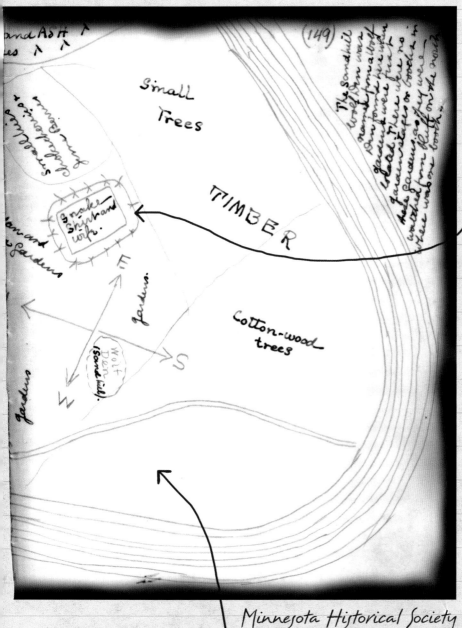

Garden plots had buck and rail fences to keep out horses and were set out 12–15 feet from the cultivated ground.

Minnesota Historical Society

All gardens in the fertile bottomlands, around
the village perimeter, were on a point that went
out into the Missouri River.

In the Garden

Gardens were used for three to four years, then allowed to lie fallow for two years.

Minnesota Historical Society

Before metal hoes, women used digging sticks to help straighten and expand the garden borders.

Dirt was mounded up around the base of the young roots to protect them from the sun.

Minnesota Historical Society

Mounds were placed a certain distance apart so the plants did not touch when they matured, ensuring large, healthy stalks.

Corn was planted on a hill, with six to eight corn stalks per hill.

Mandan Basket

The Hidatsa name for a burden basket is mi-dá-hi-si, which means "holder."

Willow wood frame

Dyed and undyed cherry bark strips woven with the plaiting technique in a triangle pattern

Leather strap, or "tumpline," placed around the forehead to bear the load

These baskets were used for carrying vegetables, holding valuable clay cooking pots while traveling from winter to summer camp, and for carrying snow into the earth lodges in winter.

Making Berry Cakes

Buffalo berries and chokecherries were pounded with a maul and berry-mashing hide, then dried in the sun for three to five days.

When enough pulp had accumulated, it was taken up in the woman's hand and made into a ball, then "squeezed out in lumps through the first finger and thumb of the right hand by pushing it with the left thumb into the right palm."
—Buffalo Bird Woman, 1916

Denver Public Library

Lakota woman making berry cakes under a sun shade, Standing Rock Reservation, North Dakota

Pemmican was also made with berries and dried meat, creating a high-protein, easy to pack food.

Gourd Ladle

Cooking and serving utensils were made from available resources.

Gourds were easily accessible for use as ladles and dippers for the Southern Plains people, much as sheep horns were accessible to the Northern Plains groups.

The gourd is of the family Cucurbitaceae, order Violales.

Cut down the center, emptied of its fleshy pulp and numerous seeds, the gourd was then allowed to dry.

Useful for serving food or water

A simple and undecorated style, but beautiful in its use of the original shape of the plant

Sheep Horn Ladle

Horns are thick at the base and taper toward the tip.

Note unusual serrated handle with hole drilled in the end.

Horns were cleaned and scraped thin, smoothed with a blade and rough stone, boiled in hot water to soften, then slit open and spread out. After hardening, the sides and handle were carved.

Horns are a hollow sheath growing over a bony core and weigh an average of 21 pounds.

Long curling horns of big horn sheep and mountain goats were a good size and shape for ladles and dippers.

Photo by Chris Gimmeson

Big Horn Sheep, *Ovis canadensis*, range the high ridges of the Rocky Mountains.

Lakota Maul

Some mauls were used to pound chokecherries, dried meat and vegetables to make different products.

Hidatsa name for stone hammer is "maopaki."

Two-thirds of the stone is covered with leather, as is the handle.

To make a maul, the stone is rounded at one end with a flat pounding face and a central groove.

A wood haft is bent around the groove, and the two ends meet to form a handle that is tied together with a leather thong.

Notes

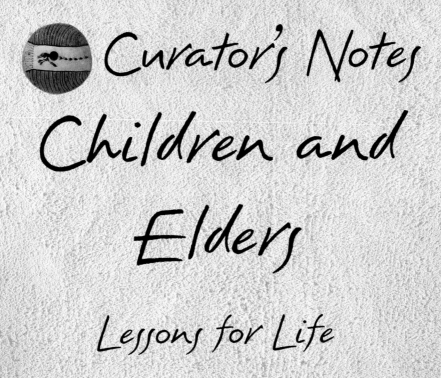

Curator's Notes

Children and Elders

Lessons for Life

Every adult in the village played a role in a child's development and education. Grandparents were especially important. They cared for the children, made them toys, and were great sources of cultural knowledge and wisdom, which they passed on through instruction, stories, and games.

Plains Indian Museum

Lakota Natal Amulet

Amulets, which held the baby's umbilical cord, were kept for a lifetime as a charm to insure a long life.

Natal amulets were attached to the cradle as a baby's first toy.

Girls had turtle amulets, and boys had lizards.

Sitting Bull

Collected from Sitting Bull, Lakota (Sioux), Fort Randall, South Dakota, 1881–1883

Turtles were part of a shared creation story of Plains groups in which the first human life was carried safely over the water-covered earth on the back of a turtle.

Crow Toy Travois

by Ben Pease

Toy depicts a fully accoutered group of riders travelling with a travois.

Painted rawhide parfleche with fringe

Feathered lance, with fur as "feathers"

Bow case and quiver

Beaded shield

Travois is loaded with belongings—drum, parfleches, and cloth bundles.

Each rider has a saddle with horse collar, crupper, stirrups and saddle bags.

Earrings

Leather dress with fringe

Beaded stirrups

Dolls

The first dolls made by Lakota and other Plains tribes were simple figures of clay or rawhide cutouts stuffed with buffalo hair or grass.

Dolls rarely had much detail in their faces, so children could imagine how they look.

Most dolls were made by elderly women as gifts for their granddaughters.

Lakota doll, 1890

A woman might keep her favorite doll for the rest of her life.

Blackfeet girl with doll; note similarities in clothing between girl and doll.

Lakota Doll

The detail in the clothing of the doll helped a girl learn her family's way of making household objects.

Dolls reflected the style of clothing in fashion at the time for a particular tribe.

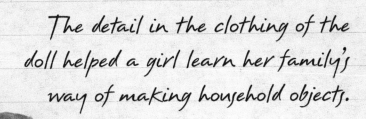

Lakota doll, 1890

With the advent of trade goods such as fabric, beads, etc., clothing became more complicated for people, as well as for dolls.

Toy Lodges

In playing with toy tipis, or lodges, girls learned to create, paint and put up a lodge, as well as how to prepare it for travel. A girl later used this skill to create and put up her own lodge.

Toy tipi cover is made of deerskin.

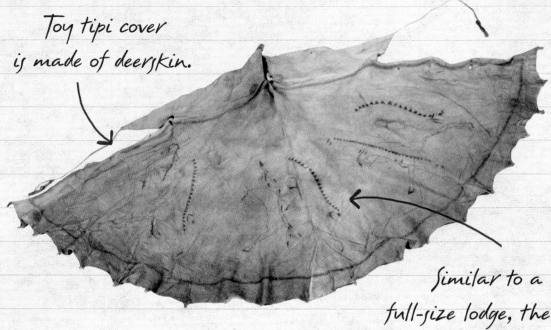

Similar to a full-size lodge, the surface of the toy tipi is painted with the images of riders on horseback.

Lakota tipis, Standing Rock Reservation, South Dakota, ca. 1890
State Historical Society of North Dakota. Photo by Frank B. Fiske

Toy Cradleboards

Girls practiced lacing their toy cradleboards and rocking dolls to sleep.

The hoop protruding from the cradle serves as a "face guard" to protect the baby.

The doll is laced into the board.

Plateau toy cradle and doll, 1890

As a baby grew older, she learned to free her arms and unlace herself from the cradle.

Kiowa girls and doll with cradleboard, ca. 1894. Oklahoma Historical Society

47

Toy Horse

Hand-tanned buckskin on body is white, perhaps so child can imagine it's their favorite color horse.

Saddle is large enough to accommodate a favorite doll.

Tail is made of horse hair.

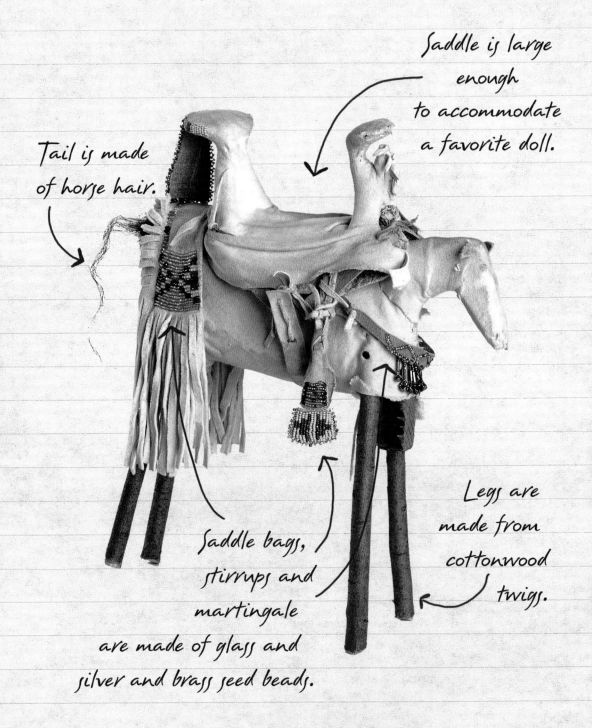

Legs are made from cottonwood twigs.

Saddle bags, stirrups and martingale are made of glass and silver and brass seed beads.

Girls and boys learned life skills from playing with toys.

Horses

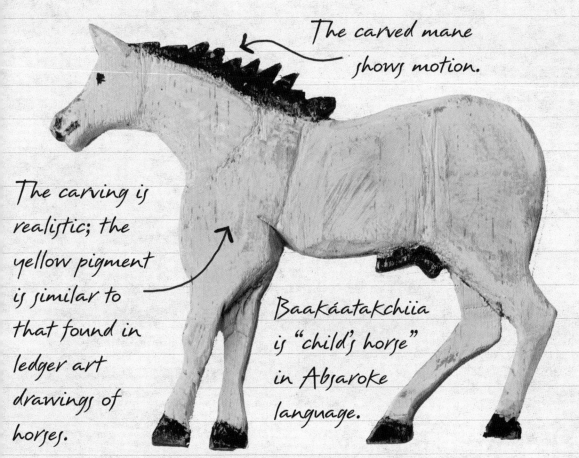

The carved mane shows motion.

The carving is realistic; the yellow pigment is similar to that found in ledger art drawings of horses.

Baakáatakchiia is "child's horse" in Absaroke language.

Historically, horses received no branding or markings. Owners identified individual horses by sight, a remarkable ability.

Crow boys on horses at Crow Indian Rodeo, Lodge Grass, Montana. July 4, 1927

Photo by W.H.D. Koerner

Notes

Curator's Notes

Women's Art

Enriching Their World

The daily tasks of quillworking, hide painting, and beadworking were vehicles of artistic expression that enriched the everyday life of the village. It was a necessity for a girl to learn these artistic skills, as it would be her measure of success as a woman. A well-dressed family and beautifully crafted home furnishings demonstrated a woman's pride and love, as well as her aptitude for economic industry within the village.

Plains Indian Museum

Porcupine Quills

The porcupine, <u>Erethizon</u> <u>dorsatum</u>, is found throughout the mountains and plains of the American West.

Wyoming Game and Fish

North American Indians were the only people in the world to use porcupine quills for art.

The length of the quill varies depending on the part of the animal from which it is taken.

The hollow quill of the porcupine is processed and dyed for quillworking.

Quillworking Techniques

Quillworking is the highest attainment of women's art.

The Lakota believe that the knowledge of porcupine quill dyeing and embroidery techniques were given to the best quillworkers in a dream from "Double Face Woman."

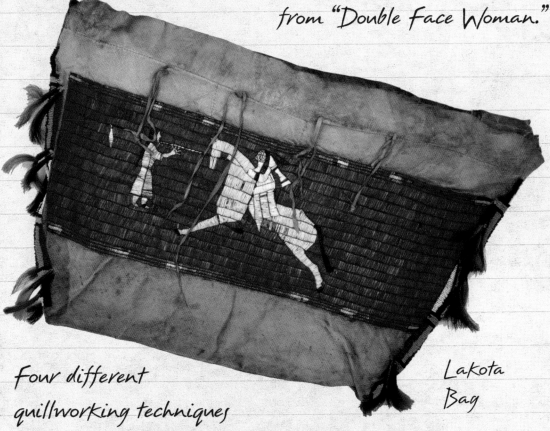

Lakota Bag

four different quillworking techniques were used to embellish personal items.

Processing the quill involved numerous steps:

- grading the quill by size,
- washing to remove natural oils,
- dyeing, using vegetable and later commercial dyes,
- softening, either in water or in the mouth, and
- flattening, by pulling the strand through the teeth

Sewn Quill Techniques

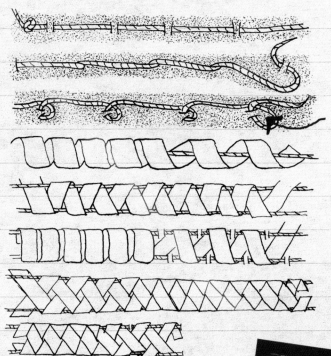

In sewn work, quills are always fastened to the surface of an object by sewing stitches.

Sewn to buckskin with sinew in rows of colorful embroidery

Hidatsa blanket strip

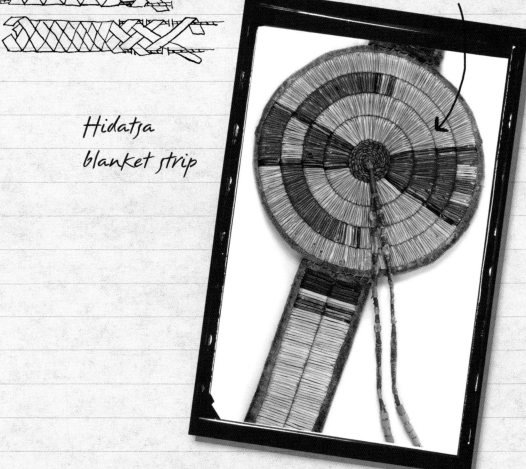

Wrapped Quill Techniques

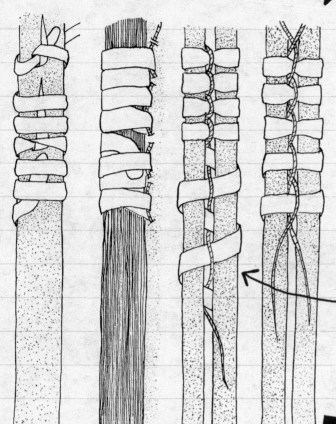

Quills are wrapped around rows of stiff rawhide to form square, stepped designs where the strips lay side by side.

This technique is typically seen on objects such as tipi ornaments.

Woven Quill Technique

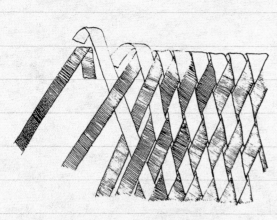

The quills are woven over and under each other to cover a wide space.

A portion of quill is first stitched down to buckskin.

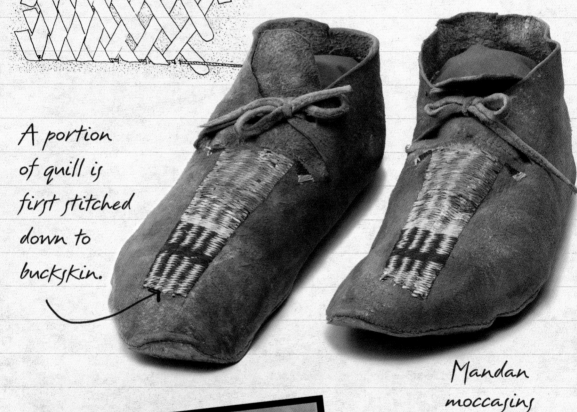

Mandan moccasins

Quillwork gives an even, shiny texture to objects.

Plaited Quill Techniques

The plaited, or braided, quill technique is done by braiding the quill with two cords of sinew.

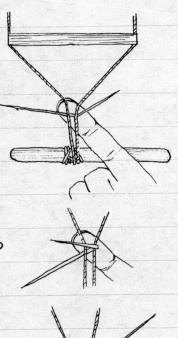

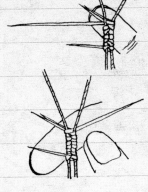

The long braid is typically wrapped around the handles of items such as a horn spoon or a pipe stem.

Two Skin & Three Skin Dresses

Older dresses were made of two hides sewn together, with the top flaps folded down in the front and back then decorated with quills or beads.

Extra hides were sometimes attached as sleeves.

Dresses maintained the same outline as the original hides.

Blackfeet "mountain sheep dress"

The third hide, or top yoke, was heavily decorated.

The tail was kept on the garment, symbolizing a woman's vitrue, elegance and grace.

Three skin dresses utilized three hides.

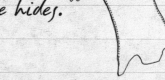

Lakota Parfleche

Fresh hide was skillfully fleshed, staked out horizontally, scraped, and washed.

Paint was mixed with hot water or glue made from beaver tails or hide scrapings.

Some of the colors used in painting included iron oxide reds, charcoal, copper carbonate green, as well as vegetable colors, such as purple from chokecherries.

With the establishment of trade with Euro-Americans, new colors were obtained.

Incising, a very old technique, was done by cutting fine lines into the damp surface of buffalo hide, then allowing the incision to dry and expand.

Notes

Curator's Notes
Buffalo

Sustenance of Life

Buffalo furnished Plains Indian people with the most important elements of life—meat for their food, hide for their clothing, robes and lodges, and bones for tools. Buffalo meat was eaten fresh, preserved by drying in the sun, or made into pemmican, a mixture of dried meat, fat, and berries. The remainder—hide, bones, hair, skull, sinews, hooves, horns, tail, paunch, and bladder—also had practical or ceremonial uses.

Plains Indian Museum

His meat sustained life:

It was cut in strips and dried, it was chopped up and packed in skins, its tallow and grease were preserved—all for winter use; its bones afforded material for implements and weapons; its skull was preserved as great medicine; its hide furnished blankets, garments, robes, and a warm and portable house; its hoofs produced glue, its sinews were used for bowstring. . . .
—Red Cloud, Lakota

Hunter Killing Buffalo, Southern Cheyenne, ca. 1890

Drying meat,
Dakota, ca. 1870
Minnesota Historical
Society

Crow Parfleche

Parfleche, an envelope made of buffalo rawhide, was used for storage and transportation and conveniently tied onto the saddle.

Diamond and triangle design with cross hatching

Stiff rawhide provides more protection than soft, tanned hides.

Heavy buffalo hide thong holds the parfleche together.

Buffalo rawhide is cut into an oblong shape, with sides folded in and top and bottom folded to meet in the middle.

Incised parfleches, from the early 19th century, probably predate those with painted designs.

Mandan Robe

Both men and women created paintings on buffalo robes.

Men generally painted scenes of hunting and warfare as a means of documenting their accomplishments.

Women primarily painted geometric designs on the robes worn by themselves and family members.

Buffalo robe painted with pigments

The Mandan described this design to Prince Maximilian as a "feather cap, under the image of the sun."

Feathered-circle or feathered-bonnet design—circles of feathers radiating out from a central figure representing the sun

Design is symbolic of a warrior's feathered bonnet.

Central sun

Circles of feathers

Northern Plains men primarily wore robes with the feathered circle design.

"Pehriska-Ruhpa/A Minataree or Big-Bellied * Indian," hand colored aquatint by Karl Bodmer, ca. 1840

*Minataree or Big Belly refers to A'anin (Gros Ventre)

65

Southern Plains Shield

Men painted their shields with sacred symbols, such as the sun, moon, stars, or animals of spiritual importance.

Holes indicate other feathers or ornaments are missing.

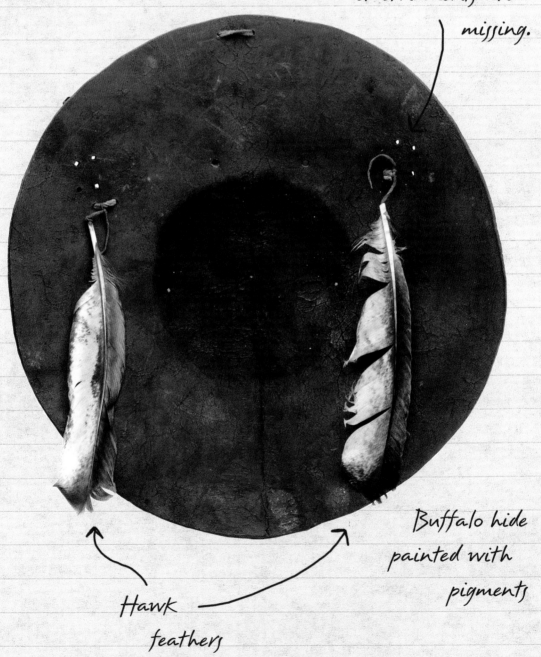

Hawk feathers

Buffalo hide painted with pigments

Men made shields from the thick hides of buffalo
bulls' necks; the hide was made thicker and
tougher by shrinking it over a fire.

Photo by Emma I. Hansen, 2000

67

Moccasins, Fort Berthold

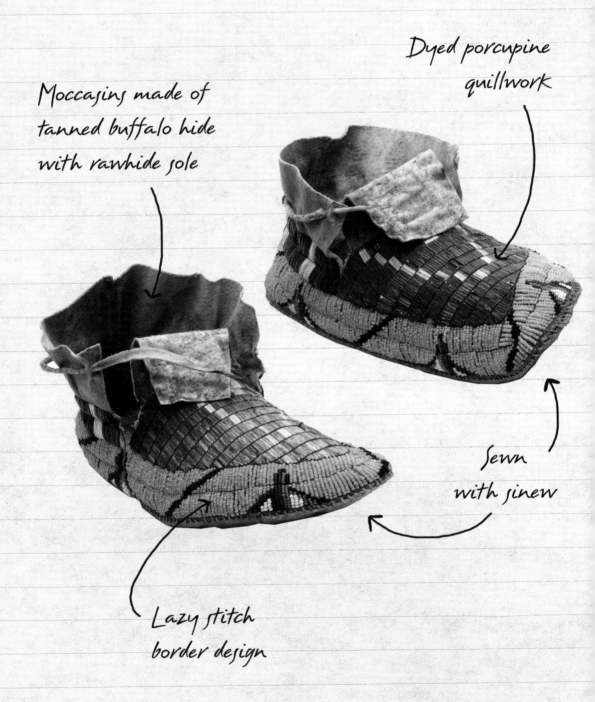

Dyed porcupine quillwork

Moccasins made of tanned buffalo hide with rawhide sole

Sewn with sinew

Lazy stitch border design

Buffalo Horn Spoons and Cup

Horn spoons, cups, and ladles were made from buffalo and mountain sheep horn and, later, cow horn.

← Cupping Horn

A spoon or ladle was made by heating the horn in a fire to clean out the inside, cutting the general outline of a spoon, boiling it to soften, then bending and shaping it.

The handle was bent and weighed down with stones.

The horn was wrapped in hide until it hardened.

The surface was smoothed, greased with animal fat, and polished by hand.

Notes

Curator's Notes

Hunting and Warfare

Sources of Honor

A man's prestige was based on his accomplishments as a warrior and hunter. Plains Indians traditionally waged war in defense or retaliation against enemy attacks, to preserve and expand hunting territories, and to capture horses, which were essential for hunting and as indicators of wealth. A man was acclaimed for his success as a hunter, and he gained war honors through a system of counting "coups," or acts of bravery against the enemy.

Plains Indian Museum

Warrior's Shirt

Warrior's shirt worn on special occasions, such as Victory dances and military society gatherings

Rosette is missing.

Painted human figures

Painted horse tracks

Shirt is constructed of two deer hides.

(Front View)

Painted horse track designs and line of human figures signify the owner's war honors.

Human figures are drawn in a simplified form, consisting of heads and torsos, characteristic of early 19th century ceremonial art.

Wool trade cloth

Upper Missouri River style is the generalized style of dress of tribes living along the Missouri River and its tributaries on the Northern Plains.

Beadwork on shoulder and arm bands consists of glass pony beads obtained through trade.

Porcupine quill-wrapped human and horse hair bundles

(Back View)

The human hair was a gift from relatives and companions, symbolizing the man's role and responsibilities as a war leader.

Glass pony beads indicate that the shirt likely was made prior to 1850 when the smaller seed beads became more readily available.

Medicine Crow

Medicine Crow
Photo by Edward S. Curtis, 1907

In all, Medicine Crow recorded 22 war deeds against the Lakota, Blackfeet, Shoshone, and Nez Perce.

Medicine Crow, whose name is more accurately translated as "Sacred Raven," was born in 1848; by the age of 22 he had completed the Crow military requirements for a chief.

- To touch or strike the first enemy fallen whether alive or dead—counting coup
- To wrestle a weapon away from an enemy
- To enter an enemy camp at night and capture a horse
- To lead a successful war party

Source: Joe Medicine Crow, _From the Heart of the Crow Country_, 1992

Crow Warrior's Shirt

After the days of Plains warfare, men living on reservations continued to wear decorated war shirts to tribal ceremonies, parades, meetings with government officials, and other events.

Beaded bands on arms and shoulders

Wool trade cloth used in rectangular neck flap

Glass seed beads available through trade after 1850

Strips of ermine, many with fur missing

Hide painted with pigment

Decorated war shirts reminded people of the man's war exploits and his continuing importance.

Northern Plains Double-Curved Bow

Bow was carved and bent to a double-curve shape while the wood was green; it was then staked on the ground for three to four days until the bow dried out enough to retain its shape.

Preferred woods for bow making: chokecherry, ash, yew, Osage orange, and hickory

Twisted sinew used for bowstring

Plains bows averaged three to four feet in length and could be easily managed from horseback; pre-horse bows were up to two feet longer.

Northern Plains Bow

Wrapped cherry bark

Some warriors of the Northern Plains, such as the Blackfeet, covered the backs of their bows with snakeskin for appearance and practical reasons.

Sinew backing is glued on the bow and covered with rattlesnake skin.

Twisted sinew bowstring

Grip wrapped with bark

Rattlesnake skin protects the sinew from moisture and fraying and strengthens the bow.

Some men excelled at bow making and were considered specialists in this craft.

Bows were often traded; among the Blackfeet, a fine bow and several arrows could be traded for a horse.

Crow Powder Measure & Lakota Powder Flask

As firearms became common on the Northern Plains, accessories often were made using new Euro-American objects and materials in innovative ways.

Brass tube wrapped with hide and decorated with beadwork

Glass bottle covered with cloth and beadwork

Cork stopper

Sitting Bull traded this flask and several other objects to the post trader, D.L. Pratt, Sr., at Fort Randall during his confinement there from 1881 to 1883.

Collected from Sitting Bull at Fort Randall, South Dakota

Pawnee Coup Stick

Coup derives from the French word meaning "blow."

Counting coup is when a warrior touches the enemy with a hand, stick, or weapon without drawing blood. The Plains warriors extolled this war deed because of the daring required in approaching the enemy closely.

A golden eagle tail feather symbolized a war honor. Eagles were admired for their courage and swiftness.

Among the Pawnee, the first man to touch the fallen enemy got the greatest honor. It was said of him, wi-ti-ki, "now he strikes."

Feats of bravery varied among tribes and included: touching a fallen enemy, killing, bringing home a scalp, capturing a horse from an enemy's camp, or leading a successful war party.

Pawnee.

White Horse, Pawnee warrior
Nebraska State Historical Society

Notes

Curator's Notes
Men's Art

Recording War Deeds and Visions

Art was integral to men's lives as warriors and hunters. Visionary experiences prepared men for war, and often inspired the designs of their shields and other equipment. Pictographs represented the land, streams, animals, plants, stars, sun, and the moon, and invoked those elements' protective powers. Men also recorded their exploits in war and hunting, as well as important tribal events, through art and oral narratives, reminding the people of their spiritual blessings.

Plains Indian Museum

Crow Shield and Cover

Painting on the shield cover depicts a bear emerging from a cave and meeting a volley of bullets.

Cover is tanned deer hide.

Earth above and below cave

Volley of bullets

Shield is buffalo rawhide.

There are four known shields painted with the same design; shields with particularly powerful designs sometimes were copied or traded.

Plain Owl owned the shield and cover, both of which were collected by Stephen G. Simms for the Field Museum of Natural History in 1902.

Flicker feather,
trade cloth, and beads

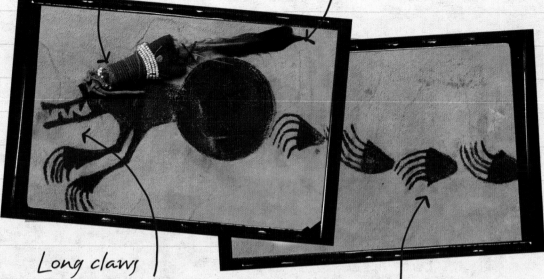

Long claws
and sharp teeth
emphasize the
danger of the bear.

Line of paw marks shows
the movement of the bear.

Wyoming Game and Fish

The grizzly bear is recognized by Plains tribes
as one of the most important and powerful creatures
among mammals, the "four-leggeds."

Gros Ventre Shield

Bull Lodge of the Gros Ventre owned this shield. The design for the shield and its cover (now lost) came to Bull Lodge in a vision.

Wool cloth, brass hawk bells, glass beads available through trade

Buffalo rawhide painted with pigments

Small bundles of herbs

Eagle and owl feathers

Bull Lodge was a great warrior and spiritual leader who, as a healer, cured gunshot wounds and many illnesses using the knowledge he received through his visions.

In 1941, Bull Lodge's daughter, Garter Snake, recounted her father's life experiences and his seven visions, including his vision about the shield, for Gros Ventre W.P.A. researcher, Fred Gone.

Crow Shield Cover

Weasel hides often decorated men's shirts, feather and horn bonnets, leggings, shields and war clubs. Weasels were admired as fierce fighting animals and known to be good war medicine.

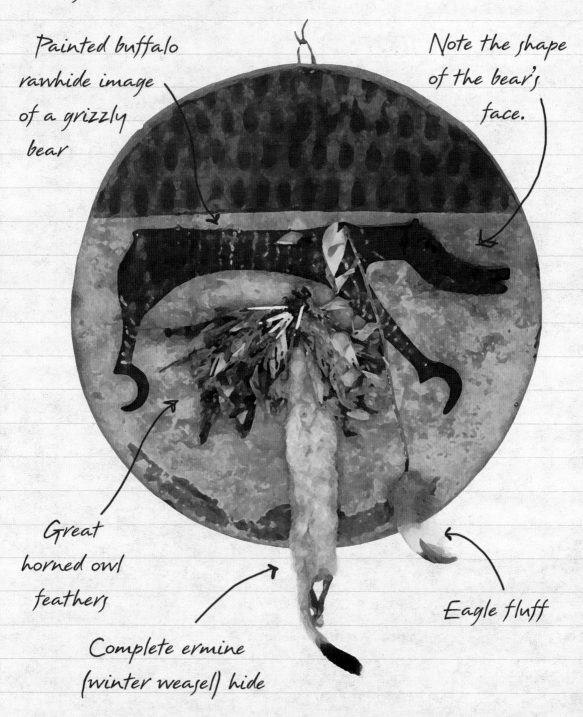

Painted buffalo rawhide image of a grizzly bear

Note the shape of the bear's face.

Great horned owl feathers

Complete ermine (winter weasel) hide

Eagle fluff

Arikara Shield and Two Covers

Red dyed feather

Shield's inner cover of tanned deer hide painted with pigments

Pieces of fur

Standing grizzly bear

The shield and two covers belonged to Fighting Bear. Anthropologist George A. Dorsey collected this set on the Arikara, Mandan, and Hidatsa reservation in North Dakota for the Field Museum of Natural History in 1903.

Fighting Bear and family
Fort Berthold, North Dakota
Montana Historical Society

Painted circle in center—the circle has important symbolic significance, as it represents the cycle of life.

Bear claws

Small medicine bundle tied to the claw

Eagle feathers painted with pigment

Shield made from buffalo rawhide

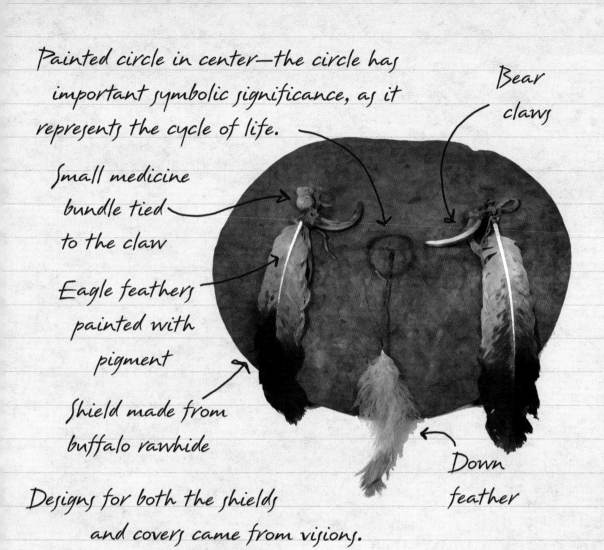

Down feather

Designs for both the shields and covers came from visions.

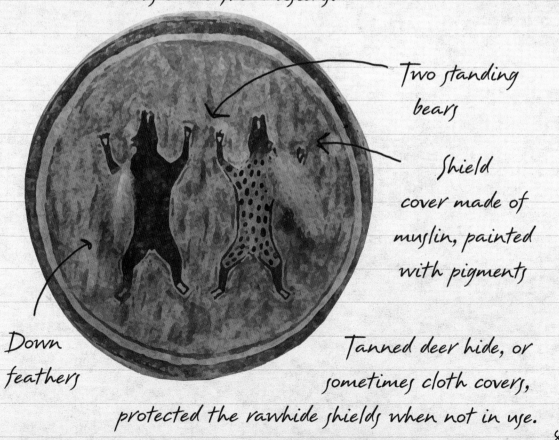

Two standing bears

Shield cover made of muslin, painted with pigments

Down feathers

Tanned deer hide, or sometimes cloth covers, protected the rawhide shields when not in use.

87

Hidatsa Shield Cover

The central figure of this shield cover is the standing bear with the claws extended and sharp teeth emphasized.

Bear is outlined in black with the color filled in.

On each side of the bear are weapons—a bow and firearm.

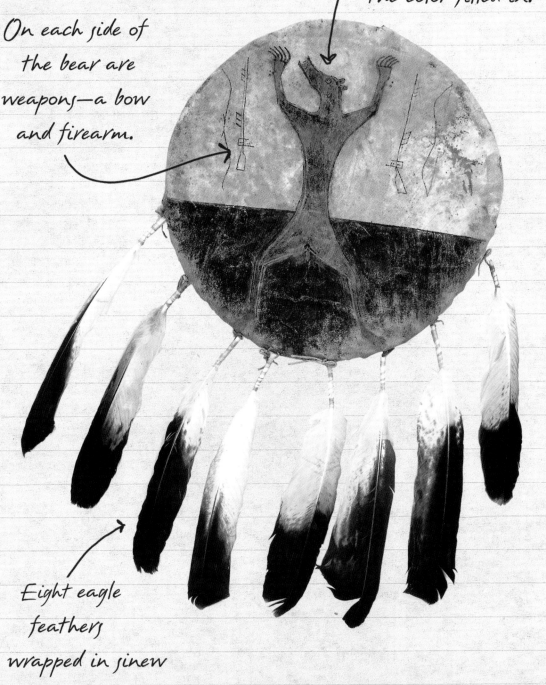

Eight eagle feathers wrapped in sinew

Lakota Dance Shield

Men depicted their personal war deeds on hide paintings, tipi covers, shields, and ledger drawings.

The Lakota warrior wears an eagle feather bonnet with a long double trailer, symbolizing his accomplishments on the battlefield.

A Lakota warrior on horseback uses a feathered staff to count coup on a standing opponent.

The opponent is armed with a rifle.

The horse is decorated for battle. His tail is tied and decorated with eagle feathers, which are also tied in his mane.

Ten eagle feathers wrapped in red cloth hang from the shield.

Horse hair

89

Notes

Curator's Notes
Sun Dance

Renewing the Circle of Life

The Sun Dance is one of the most sacred ceremonies, honoring the sun and the powers of the universe and promoting health, prosperity, and abundant buffalo herds. Participants fast, pray, and dance in a temporary lodge built around a sacred cottonwood tree. Through their suffering, they gain renewal for themselves, their families, and the earth. In 1883, the U.S. Government under the Code of Religious Offenses banned the ceremony, but it has reemerged in the 20th century with renewed significance.

Plains Indian Museum

Eagle Bone Whistle

The eagle bone whistle is used specifically in the Sun Dance ceremony, practiced by some Plains tribes.

Cord

Hollow wing bone, a natural shape for a whistle

Worn around the neck, the whistle is an important part of the Sun Dance ceremony.

Eagle plume flutters when whistle is blown.

Singing, drumming and prayer songs are part of the Sun Dance; dancers blow whistles to the beat of drums.

Lakota Eagle Bone Whistle

Hollow wing bone
of an eagle

Mouth end

Quilled medallion,
the circle symbolic of
continuity, the cycle
of life, the earth,
and the sun

Small feathers from
a flicker, a type
of North American
woodpecker

Braided buffalo
hair rope

Cheyenne Sun Dance Buffalo Skull

Skull is placed at the center pole of the Sun Dance lodge as an altar.

This treatment of the buffalo skull shows the importance of buffalo as a spirit.

Colors are symbolic: red represents warmth, blood, life and spirituality; black represents death, but also change or a transformation.

Black charcoal, from burnt wood

White clay

Red ochre, an earthy clay containing iron

Natural mineral pigments cover the surface of the skull.

Offerings to the Buffalo Spirit encourage prosperity and the return of the buffalo herds.

Construction of the Sun Dance Lodge

Twelve rafter poles support the roof, one for each month of the year.

A ceremony is held when the tree for the center pole, a forked cottonwood, is cut down, then again when it's raised for the lodge.

Lodge is round to represent the earth.

Skeleton structure of the lodge after Sun Dance is shown here.
Photo by Ken Blackbird, 1990, Rocky Boy, Montana

A buffalo head or eagle (not shown here), is suspended from the center pole; they are sacred animal spirits, key to the Plains beliefs. (This practice varies.)

Offerings to the spirits of tobacco, blankets, food, and water are placed at the base of the center pole.

After Sun Dance, the lodge is left standing to slowly fall apart, symbolically returning to the earth.

95

What is NAGPRA?

The Native American Graves Protection and Repatriation Act, or NAGPRA, is a federal law passed November 16, 1990, and applies to federal agencies, museums, educational and other institutions, and state/local governments.

NAGPRA protects burial sites and prohibits the sale or display of human remains, funerary objects, sacred objects, and objects of cultural patrimony; it also sets procedures for the return of these materials.

Sitting Bull items to be distributed

By DAVID CRISP
Of The Gazette Staff

Billings Gazette   4/29/95

Descendants of Sitting Bull have been invited to a two-day meeting in South Dakota to help determine what to do with cultural items and sacred objects associated with the Hunkpapa Sioux chief.

LaDonna Brave Bull Allard, cultural resource planner for the Standing Rock Sioux Tribe in North Dakota, said Sitting Bull may be the first Native American in the nation whose descendants have been asked to meet under the Native American Graves Protection and Repatriation Act of 1990. Eventually, she said, the process will be used to determine what to do with Native American cultural and sacred objects now in display or stored in approximately 2,000 museums in the United States.

She said she couldn't say what items associated with Sitting Bull were under consideration until the list has been turned over to the descendants. Forty-eight descendants attended meeting on the vation in So but twi this

> "We believe that if we can start with family structures and identify families so they can get back together, then there can be a healing."
>
> —LaDonna Brave Bull Allard
> Sioux Tribe planner

George Armstrong Custer at the Battle of the Little Bighorn, was killed following his arrest in 1890 Although he was a world nowned tribal leader, filling gaps in his family tree plicated problems. wives and 17 child and informa family m

Some of the objects used in the Sun Dance, a sacred ceremony, cannot be displayed; they are considered "ceremonially related" and protected under NAGPRA.

96

The return of sacred objects from well-known figures make headlines; most claims are for objects that have significance to tribes or individuals and not the general public.

▼ **BONES STORED IN WOODEN CHESTS**

Smithsonian makes inventory of Indian remains, artifacts

Museum works to give objects back to tribes

WASHINGTON (AP) — The spinal column was little more than a heap of raggedy vertebrae piled on top of each other, and the end of a darkly pitted arm bone was hugely swollen.

The Indian could not have been older than 40 when he died, and what killed him was unclear. But one diagnosis that anthropologist Allison Willcox read in the bones was certain: crippling arthritis.

With an annual budget of $1 million, researchers are quietly working to inventory thousands of Indian bones stored in wooden filing chests at the Smithsonian Institution's Museum of Natural History, best known to Americans for its dinosaur collection.

The work is part of a larger movement to repatriate to Indian tribes bones removed for scientif-ic or other reasons. The operation grew from federal laws passed in 1989 and 1990 seeking to rectify injustices against Indians by securing the return of ancestral remains and sacred, ceremonial or cultural artifacts from museums, historical societies, campuses and government agencies.

At the Smithsonian's repatriation office, bones tell individual stories but don't always shed light on tribal affiliation. Often, anthropologists must rely on other information, such as where bones were found, but even then identification is uncertain.

The arthritic Indian, for instance, is believed to have lived among the Arikara of North Dakota in the 1400s because his remains were excavated near the

(More on Objects, Page 13A)

> " Do they want a moccasin that was taken off of a baby foot? Those are questions that people really need to address. "
>
> **Elizabeth Sackler**
> Native American
> Ritual Object
> Repatriation
> Foundation

Billings Gazette 3/9/98

The Buffalo Bill Historical Center continues to work with tribes with NAGPRA inquiries and claims.

Little Chief Drawing

Little Chief's drawing, a depiction of a 19th century Sun Dance and the surrounding camp, serves as a historical record of this event in his life.

Little Chief (Koweonarre) was a Tsistsistas (Southern Cheyenne) prisoner of war, arrested in 1875 and sent to Fort Marion, Florida.

Men on vision quests on top of hills

Grazing horse herds in the distance

National Museum of the American Indian

Two boys racing their horses

Women, children and family members are not part of the ceremony in the lodge, but they participate in activities during the multi-day event.

Four warrior societies,
wearing headdresses
and performing dances, in each
of the four corners of the camp

Sweat lodges, where men
are purifying themselves
as part of the ceremony

Offering flags
flying from
the lodge's poles

Sun Dance Lodge
or Arbor in the center

Cheyenne Dog Soldiers, a warriors' society,
shown in the lower
left corner, near striped lodge

Notes

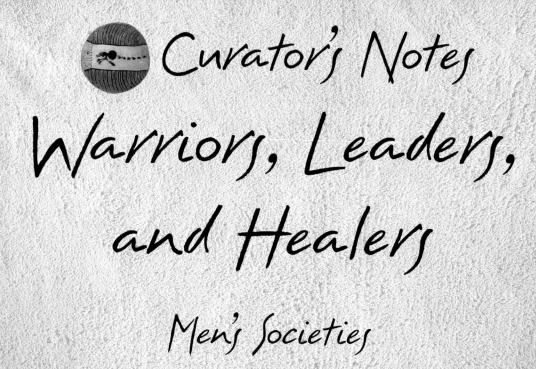

Curator's Notes

Warriors, Leaders, and Healers

Men's Societies

Men's societies prepared their members for the changing roles and responsibilities they faced throughout life. Young boys' societies trained them as warriors. Adult men's societies encouraged them to defend their tribes, territories, and resources. As a man aged he was still revered for past war honors, but reached the highest level of respect upon demonstrating his ability to be a leader, healer or peacemaker.

Plains Indian Museum

Presentation Tomahawk

Unusual combination—a non-functioning weapon and a ceremonial pipe

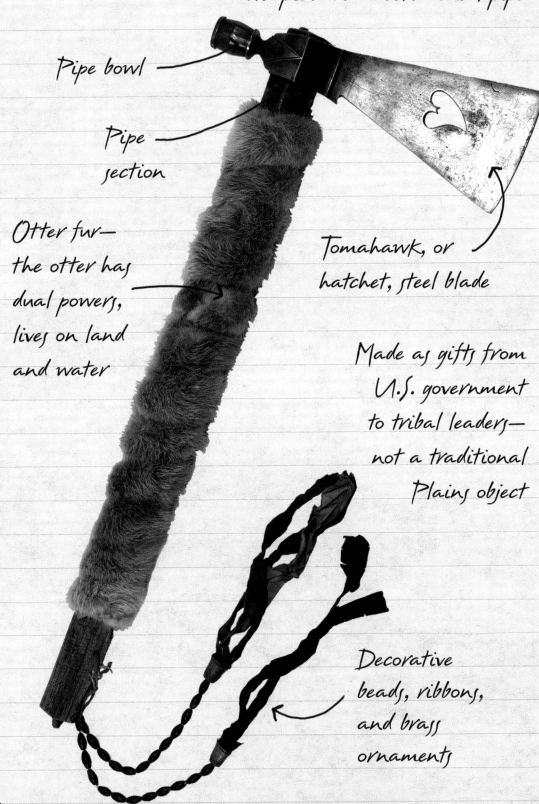

Pipe bowl

Pipe section

Otter fur— the otter has dual powers, lives on land and water

Tomahawk, or hatchet, steel blade

Made as gifts from U.S. government to tribal leaders— not a traditional Plains object

Decorative beads, ribbons, and brass ornaments

Meskwaki Bear-claw Necklace & Trailer

Claws from a sub-species of a grizzly bear, longer for digging on prairie

The necklace is an impressive object, worn by a leader to show power and importance.

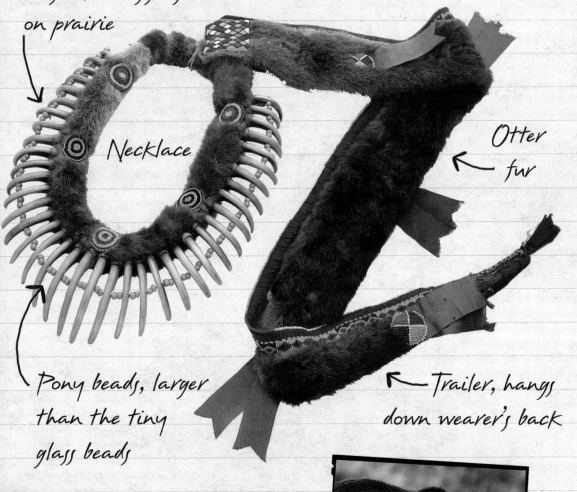

Necklace

Otter fur

Pony beads, larger than the tiny glass beads

Trailer, hangs down wearer's back

Grizzly bear claws, shorter and thicker than those on the necklace

Grizzly bear, Wyoming Game and Fish. Photo by Lu Ray Parker

Cheyenne Feather Bonnet

Bonnet— "swept back" style

The reverse side of this bonnet and trailer is as interesting as the front.

Wool "trade cloth," a trade item

Compare the materials in this bonnet, ca. 1900, to older ones.

Ribbon trim

Plains Indians believed
that eagle feathers should
never touch the ground
because the bird is sacred;
if one is dropped during
a powwow, a ceremony
is performed.

Cotton "calico" fabric,
a flowered cloth
acquired through trade

Detail from
trailer of
bonnet

The long trailer
created a dramatic
and dignified effect
whether the wearer
was standing or on
horse back.

Two Moon, Northern Cheyenne
Photo by L.A. Huffman, ca. 1880

105

Blackfeet Stand-up Feather Bonnet

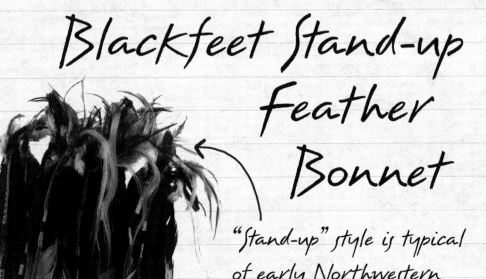

"Stand-up" style is typical of early Northwestern Plains tribes.

Sticks wrapped in quills, called "feather sticks," support feathers.

Headband and trailer are red wool "trade cloth."

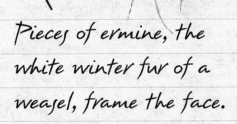

Pieces of ermine, the white winter fur of a weasel, frame the face.

Compare with later "swept back" style feather bonnets.

The shirt was more than decorative; honor was associated with the title of "shirt wearer."

Lakota Hide Shirt

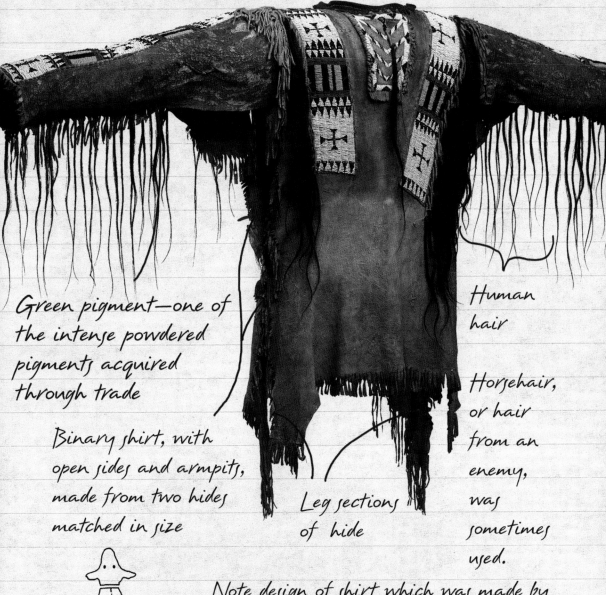

Green pigment—one of the intense powdered pigments acquired through trade

Binary shirt, with open sides and armpits, made from two hides matched in size

Human hair

Horsehair, or hair from an enemy, was sometimes used.

Leg sections of hide

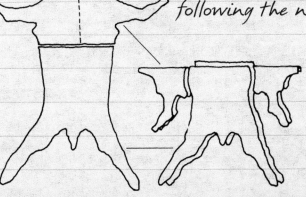

Note design of shirt which was made by following the natural shape of the hide.

Hide cut into sections— the lower part for body of shirt and the upper part for sleeves

Bald Eagle Feather

Bald Eagle Protection Act (passed in 1940) prohibits the sale, trade, purchase, transport, taking, export/import and possession of bald eagles, alive or dead, or any parts of their body, nests, or eggs.

Act was amended in 1962 to include golden eagles, and to allow Native Americans to take and use eagle feathers for religious purposes with a permit from the Secretary of the Interior.

In the early 1960s, there were fewer than 450 adult nesting pairs of bald eagles; today, there are more than 4,000.

Bald eagle feather

The bald eagle was upgraded from endangered to threatened species in 1995.

Wyoming Game and Fish
Photo by Lu Ray Parker

Golden Eagle Feather

The feathers of the bald eagle and the golden eagle, sacred rds, are used in many aspects of Indian religions and cultures.

The golden eagle is a protected species.

An unusual artifact, the golden eagle hat uses the whole head and intact wings of the golden eagle rather than single feathers.

Golden eagle feather

Photo by Charles R. Preston

Notes

Curator's Notes
Sacred Arts

Women's Societies

The sacred and ceremonial significance of the art of Plains women pervaded their everyday lives. Artistic abilities were considered gifts, often acquired through dreams or visions. Lakota, Arapaho, and Cheyenne women formed quilling and beading societies, which ensured that artistic traditions and skills would be passed on to future generations. Membership in a society, or guild, was reserved for a privileged group of talented and honorable women.

Plains Indian Museum

Quilling Societies

Quilling societies required formal initiation that included feasts and prayers.

Quilling sessions were a ceremonial act, not a hobby.

Woman quilling moccasin tops, Lakota, ca. 1893
John Anderson Collection, Nebraska State Historical Society

Techniques were passed down to younger women by experienced, older women. A young girl would have a sponsor to help her design and quill her first creation.

Men were not allowed in the tipi when a quilling session took place.

Headdress worn by Arapaho women's society honoring Buffalo Woman— a spirit figure who gives women talent to become quillworkers

Lakota Moccasins

Moccasins such as these are used for ceremonies and special occasions. Compare both moccasins; note different techniques of quillwork that create different designs.

Quilled strip attached at top and bottom

Wrapped quills— quill wrapped around a piece of hide that was attached to the moccasin

Sewn quills— hole punched with an awl, a pointed metal tool, then quill drawn through

Additional quilling techniques include plaiting around sinew thread or weaving quills.

Cheyenne Tipi Liner

Sometimes called a "dew cloth," tipi liners kept out wind, rain and snow.

Attached to inside of tipi poles with leather ties (on reverse side)

Beaded medallions

Tassels made from dew claws and dyed natural plant fibers

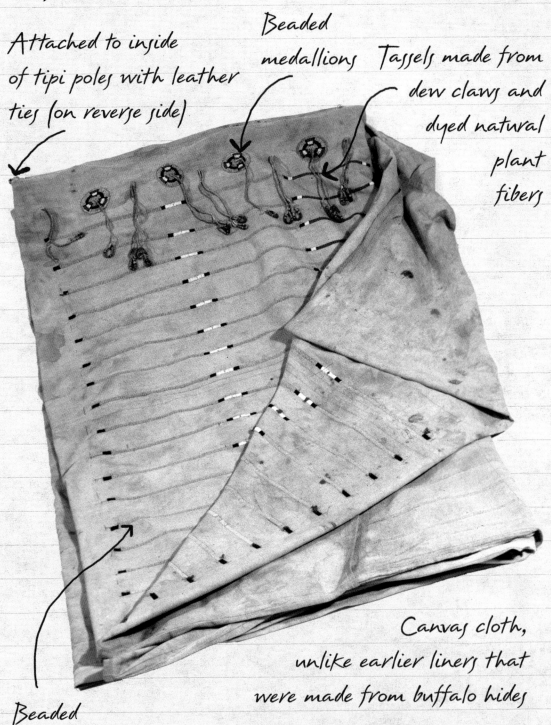

Beaded rows

Canvas cloth, unlike earlier liners that were made from buffalo hides

A tipi liner was also a decorative element for the inside of tipi.

Cheyenne Tipi Ornaments

Symbolic and decorative elements for a tipi or lodge

Circle was symbolic of the cycle of life—continuous, with no beginning and no end. Tipi is circular, and camps consist of circular groups of tipis.

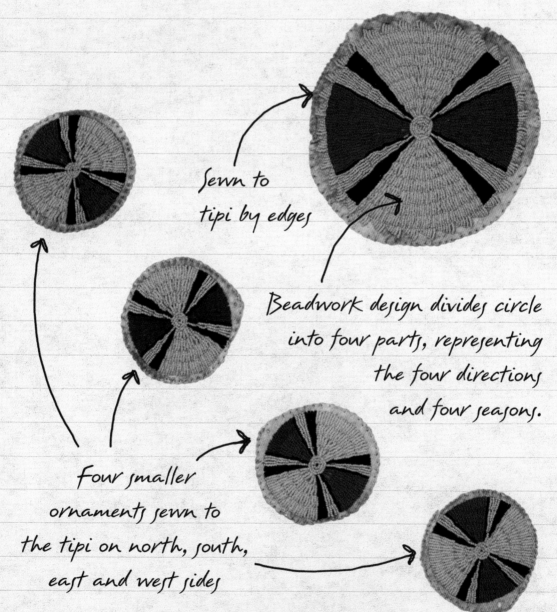

Sewn to tipi by edges

Beadwork design divides circle into four parts, representing the four directions and four seasons.

Four smaller ornaments sewn to the tipi on north, south, east and west sides

Crow Cradle

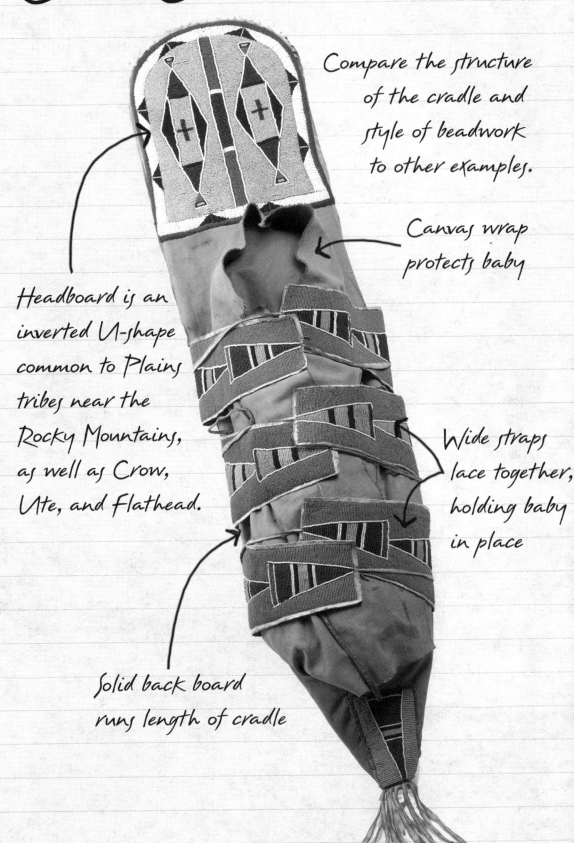

Compare the structure of the cradle and style of beadwork to other examples.

Canvas wrap protects baby

Headboard is an inverted U-shape common to Plains tribes near the Rocky Mountains, as well as Crow, Ute, and Flathead.

Wide straps lace together, holding baby in place

Solid back board runs length of cradle

This type of cradle was useful when holding a baby in one's arms or lap.

Cheyenne Cradle Hood

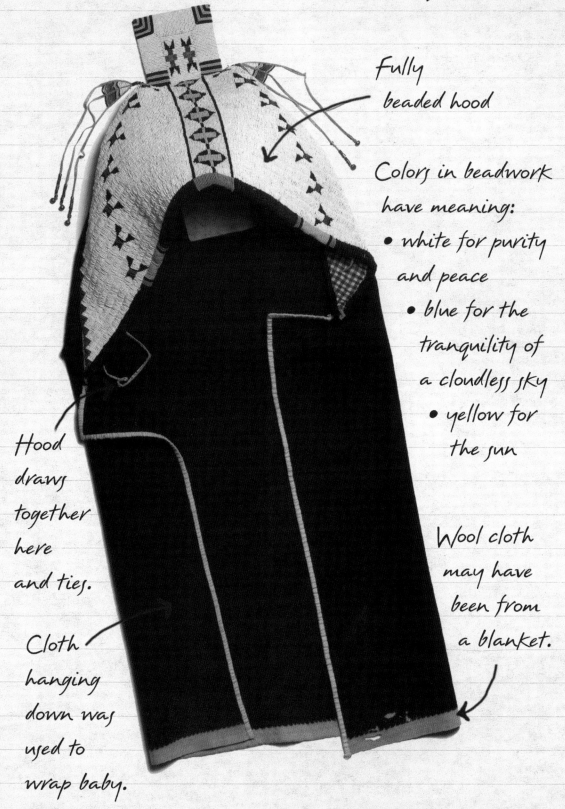

Fully beaded hood

Colors in beadwork have meaning:
- white for purity and peace
- blue for the tranquility of a cloudless sky
- yellow for the sun

Hood draws together here and ties.

Cloth hanging down was used to wrap baby.

Wool cloth may have been from a blanket.

Lakota Bladder Pouch

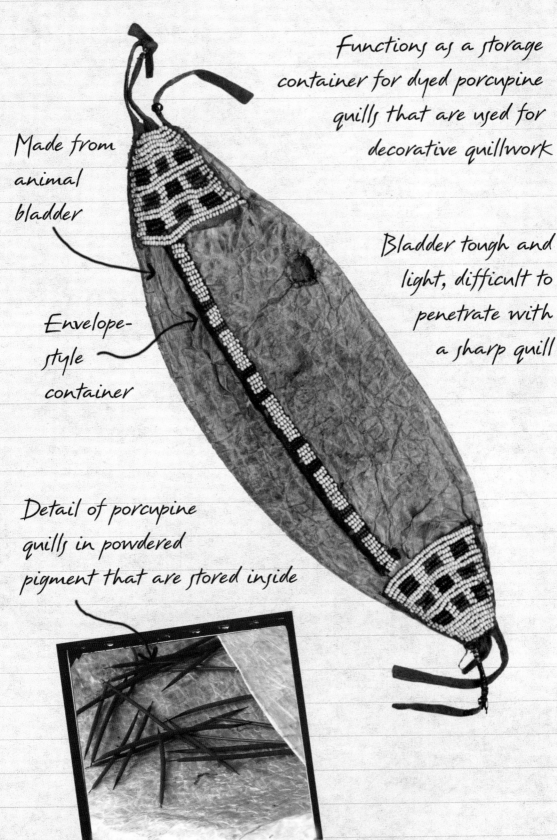

Functions as a storage container for dyed porcupine quills that are used for decorative quillwork

Made from animal bladder

Envelope-style container

Bladder tough and light, difficult to penetrate with a sharp quill

Detail of porcupine quills in powdered pigment that are stored inside

Arapaho Cradle

Design elements are symbolic:

- quilled straps represent child's ribs
- quilled disc represents child's head
- tassels represent child's hair

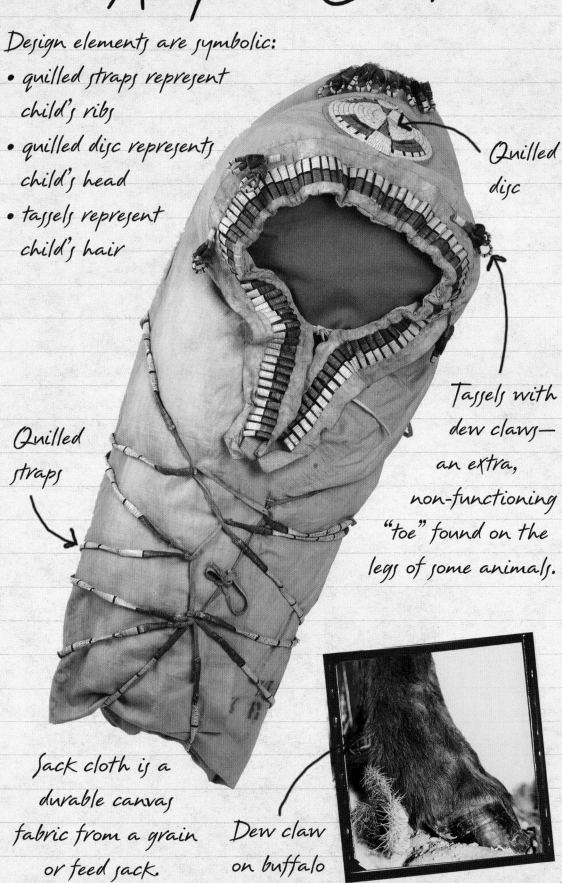

Quilled disc

Tassels with dew claws— an extra, non-functioning "toe" found on the legs of some animals.

Quilled straps

Sack cloth is a durable canvas fabric from a grain or feed sack.

Dew claw on buffalo

Notes

Curator's Notes
Ghost Dance

A Prayer for Renewal

The Ghost Dance was a powerful religious movement about hope and renewal that reached the Plains Indians in the late 1880s. The Paiute visionary Wovoka and his followers prayed for the return of their ancestors, the restoration of the great buffalo herds, and the removal of White intruders. They believed a new era would emerge for Indian people, and that the vital culture of tribal life would prevail.

Plains Indian Museum

Wovoka

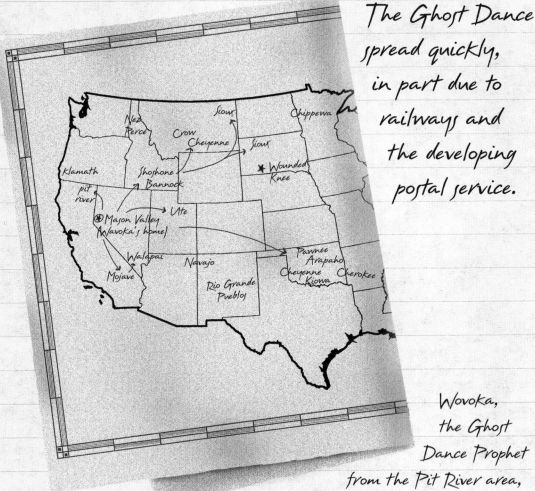

The Ghost Dance spread quickly, in part due to railways and the developing postal service.

"...Grandfather says, when your friends die you must not cry. You must not hurt anybody or do harm to anyone. You must not fight. Do right always. When the earth shakes do not be afraid. It will not hurt you."
—Wovoka, Paiute, Walker River Indian Reservation, Nevada, ca. 1891

Tobacco Bag

The crow is a sacred bird of the Ghost Dance. They are the messengers from the spirit world, their color symbolic of death and the hereafter.

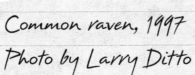

Common raven, 1997
Photo by Larry Ditto

Stand ready
Stand ready
So that when the crow calls you
So that when the crow calls you
You will see him
You will see him

—Little Raven,
Arapaho, 1891,
Ghost Dance Song

Arapaho Dress

Crescent moon on front, full moon on back

Maltese crosses symbolize the morning star and the perpetuation of life.

Red represents the morning, blue the night; the yoke appears to shift from morning to night.

Elk hide, tanned and painted with vibrant color

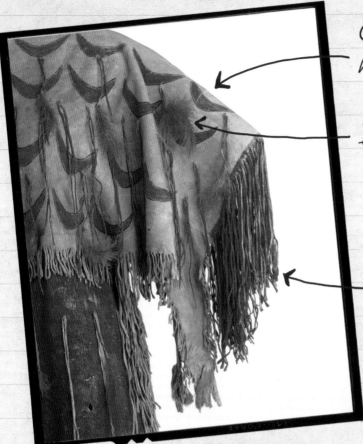

Crescent moons on half of back yoke

Dyed eagle down

Fringe painted to carry design outward

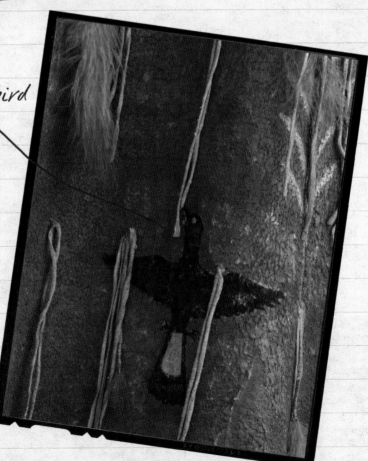

Crows, magpies and the thunderbird are important Ghost Dance symbols; the thunderbird is the spiritual manifestation of the eagle.

Lakota Shirt

Wovoka supplied red ochre to Ghost dancers,
via traveling emissaries, for use on clothing and bodies.

One piece of
muslin,
folded
at the
shoulder

Eagle feathers are attached
by folding the feather quill back on itself,
around cotton string; the point is then inserted
into the stem of the hollow quill.

Fringe attached around yoke
and at neck opening

Red pigment rubbed
into fringe and neckline

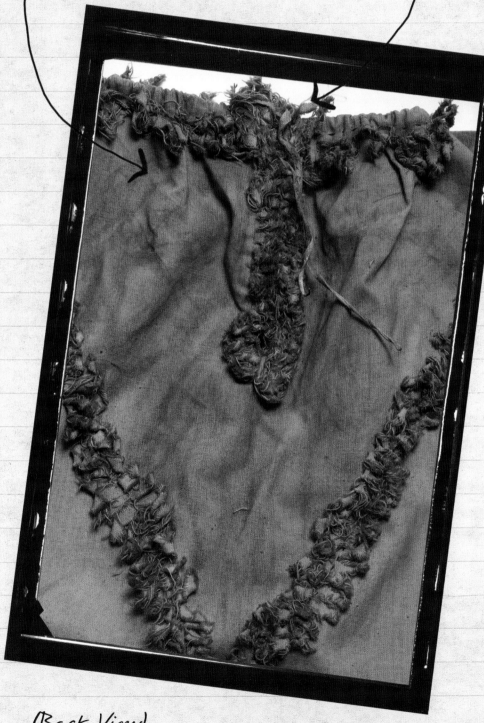

(Back View)

Arapaho Dress

Colorful ribbons, ermine tails and feet, and feathers are powerful icons of the earth and sky.

Astral imagery—five pointed stars—reflects hope for the dawn of a new era.

Hawk bells are attached to side fringes.

Blue represents the night.

Fully painted deer hide

Horizontal stripe divides dress into two—the earth and the sky.

Wounded Knee

Site of the Wounded Knee Massacre of 1890, Denver Public Library

"...These people were coming toward Pine Ridge agency, and when they were almost on the agency they were met by the soldiers and surrounded and finally taken to the Wounded Knee Creek... their guns were demanded... men were separated from their families, from the tipis... A young man... among that bunch of Indians fired his gun, and of course the firing of a gun must have been the breaking of a military rule... immediately the soldiers returned fire and indiscriminate killing followed."
—Turning Hawk, report to the Commissioner of Indian Affairs, 1891

Wounded Knee Cemetery, 1990 Photo by Robert Weiglein

Notes

Curator's Notes
Reservation Art

Traditions in Transition

Beginning in the 1870s, Plains Indians were denied access to ancestral lands, dislodged from established economies, and tutored in Christian ideologies, their sacred traditions prohibited by law. Yet Plains people sustained their cultural identities, in part through the production of art. Objects and imagery of this era celebrated tribal affiliations, honored traditions, and evolved to accommodate an altered world. Reservation-era art is a testament to Plains Indian vitality and dynamism in the face of adversity.

Plains Indian Museum

Lakota Dress

Three-skin dress with heavily beaded yoke and long fringe at sleeves, worn for special occasions

In the early reservation period of the 1890s, women began using pictorial designs in their beadwork.

Weighty, beaded yoke is balanced by successive rows of fringe, beadwork, and tassels, as well as cones and beaded tabs.

The back of the dress is as elaborate as the front.

Horse motifs break free of ordered rows of lazy stitch.

Twill-woven wool cloth,
one of many kinds of trade cloth
available on the Northern Plains,
was a good choice for dresses.

Blackfeet Dress

Silk ribbon
binding

Strands of
tubular
glass trade
beads with
a hawk bell
or thimble
at the end
of each

Brass beads
stitched in rows,
with a pattern
that dips at the
yoke like earlier
deer-tail or
two-skin dresses

Silk binds hem

Appliqué stripes
of silk ribbons,
hand sewn in place

133

Crow Moccasins

Crow beadworkers began to use floral designs around the 1890s; by the 1920s, floral patterns had nearly replaced geometric, although alternating triangles are used as a border here.

Large flaps extend up the leg and wrap around ankles for added warmth, a style suited to Northern Plains.

Soft soles of deer hide

Roses—solitary motifs with dark lines for contour

Overlay beadwork covers the entire surface of uppers, made of soft deer hide.

Kiowa Moccasins

These moccasins show the use of pigment, long fringes, and sparsely applied beadwork, characteristic of Southern Plains decoration.

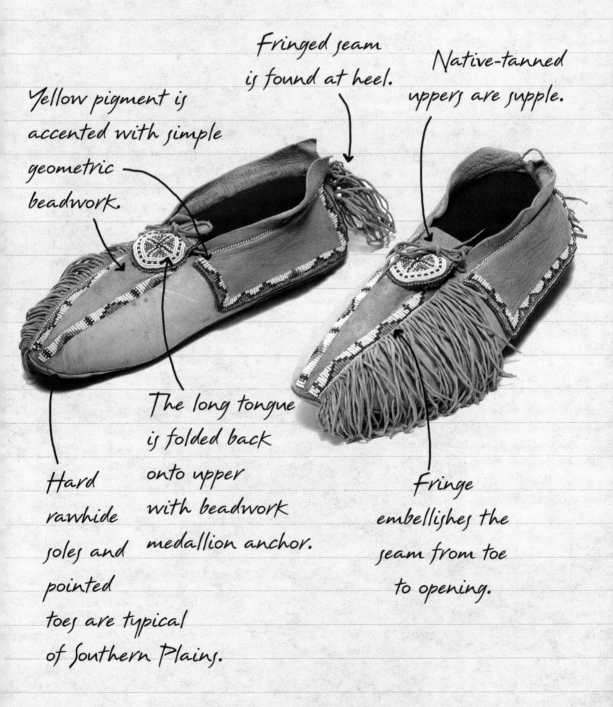

Fringed seam is found at heel.

Native-tanned uppers are supple.

Yellow pigment is accented with simple geometric beadwork.

The long tongue is folded back onto upper with beadwork medallion anchor.

Hard rawhide soles and pointed toes are typical of Southern Plains.

Fringe embellishes the seam from toe to opening.

Crow Shirt

A "binary" shirt is made from two hides of equal size—body and hind leg skins form the shirt body, forelegs and upper body skins form the sleeves.

Red wool cloth is the foundation for beadwork, but it becomes integral to the design.

Beaded bands cover seams and become important decorative elements.

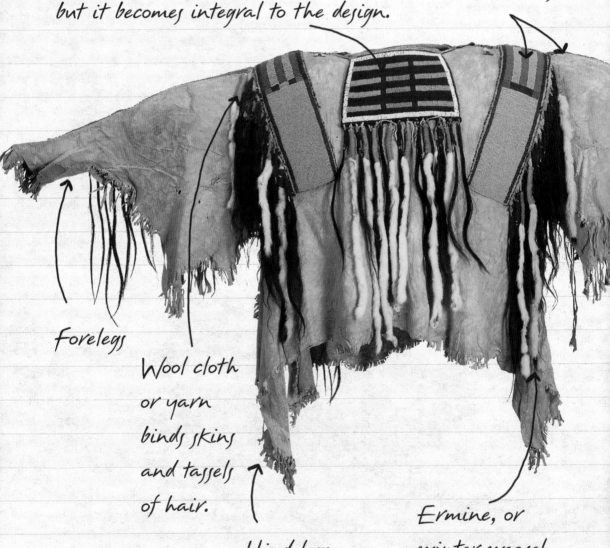

Forelegs

Wool cloth or yarn binds skins and tassels of hair.

Hind legs of deer skin

Ermine, or winter weasel skins, with black tail tips

Meskwaki Turban

Beadwork:

- Overlay stitch anchors colorful background shapes.
- Hand and borders are outlined.
- Outside edges incorporate netted beadwork.

Beadwork border with red cotton cloth lining and top

White-tail deer hair and red feather tassel

Eagle feather and eagle down

German Silver bear paw, worn together w/bearclaw necklace, signifies high status.

Beadwork binding

Otter fur trailer with fur on the inside surface and elaborate beadwork on the outside

John Young Bear wears a bearclaw necklace and this turban of his own making.

Blackfeet Gun Case

Overlay beadwork produces a smooth, dense surface.

Diamond and triangles with edges smoothed out

Well-tanned hide fringe

Stacked, stepped, geometric designs, prominent in Blackfeet beadwork

Diagonal stripes appear as borders on gun cases.

Sense of identity and achievement through adornment

Medicine Owl, Blackfeet, ca. 1910. Photo by Roland Reed

Lakota Bag

Border of triangles replicates the shape of the cone tassels.

Reverse side is unadorned, except for vertical beadwork bands at left and right edges.

Tassels are dyed red feathers, tin cones, and glass beads.

Tin cones made from snuff cans and other sources of tin

One green bugle bead

Plains beadwork of the transitional period often includes flags, appropriated icons of power.

Notes

Curator's Notes

Plains Indian Art Today

Contemporary Expressions

Plains art is produced in a diverse range of media and takes many forms, from the conventional to the avant garde. With respect for what has come before, an understanding of the present, and an eye to the future, Plains Indian artists interpret, and reinterpret, their experience as Indian people. They create art that honors ancestral creativity and ingenuity, celebrates cultural ideals and tribal identity, and transcends time and place.

Plains Indian Museum

Saddle by Marcus Dewey, Arapaho

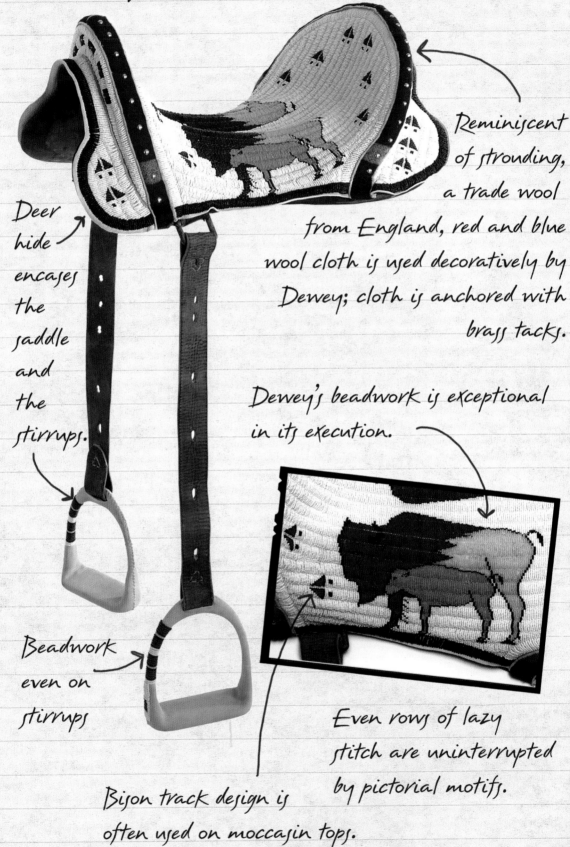

Reminiscent of strouding, a trade wool from England, red and blue wool cloth is used decoratively by Dewey; cloth is anchored with brass tacks.

Deer hide encases the saddle and the stirrups.

Dewey's beadwork is exceptional in its execution.

Beadwork even on stirrups

Even rows of lazy stitch are uninterrupted by pictorial motifs.

Bison track design is often used on moccasin tops.

Kiowa Cradle

by Vanessa Jennings

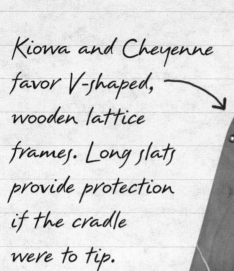

Kiowa and Cheyenne favor V-shaped, wooden lattice frames. Long slats provide protection if the cradle were to tip.

Asymmetrical color use— blue on one side, yellow on the other

Jennings uses vivid colors for both beads and hide.

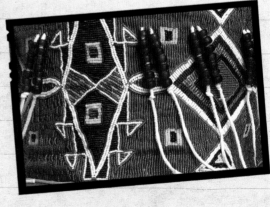

Kiowa cradles combine geometric and abstract floral designs. This cradle is based on a family design.

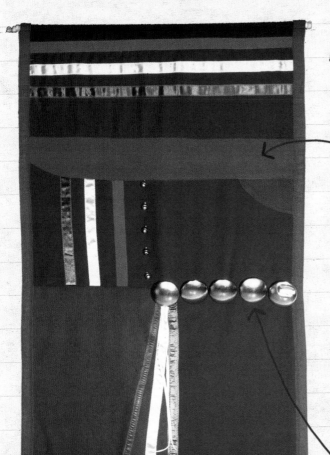

Banner

by Arthur Amiotte,
Lakota

Part of a series of
works that celebrates
the collaborative
nature of Plains
art—inspired by
transitional
period dresses

German silver
conchos on belts

Red and blue trade
cloth of wool made
beautiful dresses;
ribbons were applied
for embellishment
on sleeves and hems.

Native American women cooking outdoors
Denver Public Library

Lakota High Tops

Approaches vary in contemporary beadwork, from traditional forms and styles to all new objects, each unique.

Simple overlay patterns, lightly beaded

Fully beaded in lazy stitch

Turquoise canvas of commercial high tops is integral to design.

Lakota sneakers

Chippewa-Cree Ball

An ordinary tennis ball is the foundation, a surprising use of materials.

Pearlescent and iridescent beads are relatively new options for today's beadworkers.

Turtles, often the animal representation of the earth, are significant for many tribes.

Embroidering on an orb is very difficult; overlay stitch anchors the beads snuggly.

Dakota Bustle

Long and showy feathers are used for dance regalia—pheasant feathers in this case.

Brightly dyed downy feathers encircle a beaded medallion.

A combination of feather lengths are built up in layers for a full circle that sways with movement.

Trailer is a strip of blanket fabric.

Radiating circles are a recurring form—star quilts, feathers, bonnets, and bustles.

Dancers at Plains Indian Powwow, 1998
Photo by Devendra Shrikhande

147

Beaded Vest

During the early reservation period, women began producing beaded vests for male family members to wear for special occasions. Men today wear such vests at powwow, parades, and tribal celebrations.

The Shoshone rose beadwork pattern became prevalent after World War II.

Faceted beads

Contemporary beadwork features both geometric and floral designs.

Vest by Debra Lee (Stone) Jay, Shoshone-Bannock, 2002

Southern Plains Peyote Fan

Contemporary artists reflect tradition and innovation in their religious art.

Fans combine feathers of colorful birds, such as the pheasant and macaw feathers used here.

Clipped feathers

Comanche artist Ginger Otipoby makes Native American Church jewelry, often depicting water birds who carry prayers heavenward.

Plied leather fringe

The Native American Church is highly individualistic, as are the art forms it inspires.

Notes

Curator's Notes Acknowledgements

All objects are from the collections of the Buffalo Bill Historical Center, Cody, Wyoming, unless otherwise noted.

Page 2: Gros Ventre Parfleche Case, Chandler-Pohrt Collection, Gift of Mr. and Mrs. Richard A. Pohrt. NA.106.210A

Page 3: Crow Cylinder Case, Chandler-Pohrt Collection, Gift of PacifiCorp Foundation. NA.106.595.2

Page 4: Photo by Edward S. Curtis, *The North American Indian*; . . .*of the United States and Alaska*. [Seattle Wash.][Cambridge, U.S.A., E.S. Curtis; The University press], 1907–1930. RB.TR.647.C87-1907.PV.pl105.

Page 4: Photo by Edward S. Curtis, *The North American Indian*; . . .*of the United States and Alaska*. RB.TR.647.C87-1907.PIII.pl105.

Page 5: Shoshone Winter Moccasins, Chandler-Pohrt Collection, Gift of Mr. and Mrs. Alan S. McDowell. NA.202.889

Page 6: Blackfeet Capote, Chandler-Pohrt Collection, Gift of Mr. William D. Weiss. NA.202.481

Page 7: Crow Bowcase and Quiver. NA.102.125

Page 8: Crow Storage Bag, In memory of Frank O. Horton and Henriette S. Horton. NA.106.648

Page 9: Lakota Trunk, The Irving H. "Larry" Larom Collection. NA.106.11.

Page 9: Photo by Edward S. Curtis, *The North American Indian*. . . .*of the United States and Alaska*. RB.TR.647.C87-1907, vol. 6, p.6.

Page 12: Upper Missouri River Saddle Blanket, Chandler-Pohrt Collection. NA.403.164

Page 13: Cree Pad Saddle, Gift of Mrs. F.W. Watrous. The Colonel John F. Guilfoyle, U.S. Calvary, West Point 1877, Collection of American Indian Material. NA.403.97

Page 14: Crow Girl's Saddle, Gift of the Irving Hastings Larom Estate. NA.403.102

Page 15: Crow Bridle. NA.403.47

Page 16: Crow Crupper, Gift of the Irving Hastings Larom Estate. NA.403.36

Page 17: Crow Saddlebags, Gift of the Irving Hastings Larom Estate. NA.403.65

Page 18: Lakota Saddlebags, Catherine Bradford McClellan Collection, Gift of The Coe Foundation. NA.403.10

Page 19: Lakota Bag (front and back), Gift of Corliss C. and Audrienne H. Moseley. NA.203.437

Page 19: Lakota Pipe Bowl and Stem, Gift of J.W. Duke Wellington. NA.504.163A/B

Page 22: Hairpipe Necklace, Catherine Bradford McClellan Collection, Gift of The Coe Foundation. NA.203.234

Page 22: Assiniboine woman, photo, Gift of Robert S. Crichton. P.40.1

Page 23: Upper Missouri Leggings, Chandler-Pohrt Collection, Gift of Mr. William D. Weiss. NA.202.440

Page 24: Arikara Rattle, Chandler-Pohrt Collection, Gift of Mr. William D. Weiss. NA.505.26

Page 25: Lakota Rifle Case, Gift of Mr. H. Peter Kriendler. NA.102.5

Page 26: Lakota Knife and Case. NA.102.91A/B

Page 27: Four Point Hudson's Bay Blanket, Chandler-Pohrt Collection, Gift of Mr. William D. Weiss NA.202.449

Page 27: Photo by Roland Reed, (detail). P.43.54

Page 27: Capote, Adolf Spohr Collection, Gift of Larry Sheerin. NA.202.214

Page 28: Bone Hair Pipes (detail) on Lakota Breastplate, Adolf Spohr Collection, Gift of Larry Sheerin. NA.203.236

Page 28: Dentalium Shells (detail) on Lakota Dress, Gift of Mr. Robert Garland. NA.202.40

Page 35: Mandan Basket, Chandler-Pohrt Collection, Gift of Mr. William D. Weiss. NA.106.183

Page 37: Gourd Ladle. NA.106.469

Page 38: Sheep Horn Ladle. NA.106.15

Page 39: Lakota Maul, Chandler-Pohrt Collection, Gift of Mr. William D. Weiss. NA.106.330

Page 42: Lakota Natal Amulet. NA.502.24

Page 42: Sitting Bull, photo, Gift of Mr. & Mrs. Gerorge Strobel. P.6.38

Page 43: Crow Toy Travois, The Crow Indian Collection of Dr. William and Anna Petzoldt, Gift of Genevieve Petzoldt Fitzgerald. NA.507.69

Page 44: Lakota Doll, Chandler-Pohrt Collection, Gift of Mr. William D. Weiss. NA.507.64

Page 45: Lakota Doll, Chandler-Pohrt Collection, Gift of Mr. William D. Weiss. NA.507.66

Page 46: Toy Tipi Cover, Chandler-Pohrt Collection, Gift of Mr. William D. Weiss. NA.507.58

Page 47: Plateau Toy Cradle and Doll. NA.507.83

Page 48: Toy Horse, Simplot Collection, Gift of J.R. Simplot. NA.507.90

Page 49: Toy Horse. NA.507.16

Page 49: Photo by W.H.D. Koerner, Gift of the artist's heirs, W.H.D. Koerner, III, and Ruth Oliver Koerner. P.78.4377

Page 52: Porcupine Quills, Loan from Mr. William P. Fitzgerald. L.35.95.5

Page 53: Lakota Bag, Chandler-Pohrt Collection, Gift of Mr. William D. Weiss. NA.106.245

Page 54: Hidatsa Blanket Strip (detail), Chandler-Pohrt Collection, Gift of the Pilot Foundation. NA.203.396

Page 56: Mandan Moccasins, Chandler-Pohrt Collection, Gift of Friends of James Nielson and Anne Young in honor of their marriage. NA.202.461

Page 57: Quilled Spoon Handle (detail), Chandler-Pohrt Collection, Gift of Mr. William D. Weiss. NA.106.182

Page 58: Blackfeet Mountain Sheep Dress, Gift of Mrs. Henry H.R. Coe. NA.202.376

Page 59: Lakota Parfleche, The Irving H. "Larry" Larom Collection. NA.106.234.1

Page 59: Incised Parfleche (detail), Chandler-Pohrt Collection, Gift of the Robert S. and Grayce B. Kerr Foundation, Inc. NA.106.594

Page 62: Galloping, Littleman, Kiowa or Sweetwater; Southern Cheyenne, *Untitled (Indian man on horse shooting arrow in buffalo)*, December 1894–January 1895, pencil, ink and crayon on paper, 5.625 x 8.625 in. Gift of Mr. and Mrs. Joseph M. Katz. 48.59.13

Page 63: Crow Parfleche, Chandler-Pohrt Collection, Gift of the Robert S. and Grayce B. Kerr Foundation, Inc. NA.106.594

Page 64: Mandan Robe, Chandler-Pohrt Collection, Gift of Mr. William D. Weiss. NA.202.839

Page 65: Karl Bodmer, artist (1809–1893). Paul Legrand, engraver. *Pehriska-Ruhpa/A Minataree or Big-Bellied Indian*, ca. 1840–1843, aquatint (hand-colored), 24.875 x18.125 in. Gift of Clara S. Peck. 21.69.37

Page 66: Southern Plains Shield, Adolf Spohr Collection, Gift of Larry Sheerin. NA.502.18

Page 68: Moccasins, Fort Berthold, Gift of Harriet D. Reed and Betty N. Landercasper in memory of W. Guruea Dyer. NA.202.137

Page 69: Cupping Horn, Chandler-Pohrt Collection, Gift of Mr. and Mrs. Richard A. Pohrt. NA.106.217

Page 69: Spoon (left). NA.106.27

Page 69: Spoon (right). NA.106.316

Page 72: Warrior's Shirt, Chandler-Pohrt Collection, Gift of Mr. William D. Weiss. NA.202.486

Page 74: Photo by Edward S. Curtis, *The North American Indian; . . . of the United States and Alaska*. RB.TR.647.C87-1907.PIV.pl117.

Page 75: Crow Warrior's Shirt, Gift of Harriet D. Reed and Betty N. Landercasper in memory of W. Guruea Dyer. NA.202.773

Page 76: Northern Plains Double-Curved Bow, The Irving H. "Larry" Larom Collection. NA.102.62

Page 77: Northern Plains Bow, Simplot Collection, Gift of J.R. Simplot. NA.102.157

Page 78: Crow Powder Measure, Chandler-Pohrt Collection, Gift of Mr. William D. Weiss. NA.102.94

Page 78: Lakota Powder Flask. NA.102.137

Page 79: Pawnee Coup Stick, Chandler-Pohrt Collection, Gift of Mr. and Mrs. Richard A. Pohrt. NA.108.32

Page 82: Crow Shield and Cover, Chandler-Pohrt Collection, Gift of Mr. and Mrs. Edson W. Spencer. NA.108.105

Page 84: Gros Ventre Shield, Collection of Richard and Marian Pohrt. L.8.87.25

Page 85: Crow Shield Cover, Adolf Spohr Collection, Gift of Larry Sheerin. NA.108.13

Page 86: Arikara Shield Cover, Adolf Spohr Collection, Gift of Larry Sheerin. NA.108.14

Page 87: Arikara Shield, Adolf Spohr Collection, Gift of Larry Sheerin. NA.502.66

Page 87: Arikara Shield Cover, Adolf Spohr Collection, Gift of Larry Sheerin. NA.108.13

Page 88: Hidatsa Shield Cover, Adolf Spohr Collection, Gift of Larry Sheerin. NA.108.17

Page 89: Lakota Dance Shield, Gift of Corliss C. and Audrienne H. Moseley. NA.502.3

Page 92: Eagle Bone Whistle, Adolf Spohr Collection, Gift of Larry Sheerin. NA.505.8

Page 93: Lakota Eagle Bone Whistle, Chandler-Pohrt Collection, Gift of Mr. and Mrs. Richard A. Pohrt. NA.502.97

Page 94: Cheyenne Sun Dance Buffalo Skull, Gift of Anne T. Black. NA.502.35

Page 102: Presentation Tomahawk, Adolf Spohr Collection, Gift of Larry Sheerin. NA.504.127

Page 103: Meskwaki Bear-claw Necklace and Trailer, Adolf Spohr Collection, Gift of Larry Sheerin. NA.203.213

Page 104: Cheyenne Feather Bonnet. NA.205.9

Page 105: Photo by L.A. Huffman, Gift of Thomas Minckler. P.100.1950

Page 106: Blackfeet Stand-up Feather Bonnet, Chandler-Pohrt Collection, Gift of Mr. and Mrs. Richard A. Pohrt. NA.203.357

Page 106: Northern Plains Feather Bonnet. NA.205.47

Page 107: Lakota Hide Shirt. NA.202.205

Page 109: Eagle Hat, The Irving H. "Larry" Larom Collection. NA.203.168

Page 112: Buffalo Society Headdress, Chandler-Pohrt Collection, Gift of Mr. William D. Weiss. NA.203.358

Page 113: Lakota Moccasin (upper). NA.202.7

Page 113: Lakota Moccasin (lower), The Irving H. "Larry" Larom Collection. NA.202.6

Page 114: Cheyenne Tipi Liner. NA.302.25

Page 115: Cheyenne Tipi Ornaments. NA.302.18A-E

Page 116: Crow Cradle, Adolf Spohr Collection, Gift of Larry Sheerin. NA.111.17

Page 117: Cheyenne Cradle Hood, Gift of Mr. and Mrs. J. Whitney King, Jr. NA.111.20

Page 118: Lakota Bladder Pouch, Chandler-Pohrt Collection, Gift of Mr. William D. Weiss. NA.106.283

Page 119: Arapaho Cradle, Chandler-Pohrt Collection, Gift of Mr. William D. Weiss. NA.111.47

Page 123: Tobacco Bag, Chandler-Pohrt Collection, Gift of Mr. William D. Weiss. NA.504.305

Page 124: Arapaho Dress, Chandler-Pohrt Collection, Gift of Mary J. and James R. Jundt. NA.204.4

Page 126: Lakota Shirt, Gift of The New Hampshire Historical Society. NA.204.2

Page 128: Arapaho Dress, Gift of Mr. J.C. Kid Nichols. NA.204.1

Page 132: Lakota Dress, Gift of Mr. and Mrs. William Henry Harrison. NA.202.70

Page 133: Blackfeet Dress, Chandler-Pohrt Collection, Gift of Mr. and Mrs. Charles W. Duncan, Jr. NA.202.466

Page 134: Crow Moccasins, The Irving H. "Larry" Larom Collection. NA.202.152

Page 135: Kiowa Moccasins, Gift of Richard W. Leche. NA.202.20

Page 136: Crow Shirt, Adolf Spohr Collection, Gift of Larry Sheerin. NA.202.351

Page 137: Meskwaki Turban, Adolf Spohr Collection, Gift of Larry Sheerin. NA.205.16

Page 137: John Young Bear, photo, Adolf Spohr Collection, Gift of Larry Sheerin. P.42.36

Page 138: Blackfeet Gun Case, Chandler-Pohrt Collection, Gift of Mr. William D. Weiss. NA.102.87

Page 138: Photo by Roland Reed. P.43.30

Page 139: Lakota Bag, Gift of Corliss C. and Audrienne H. Moseley. NA.109.72

Page 142: Saddle by Marcus Dewey, Museum purchase with funds provided by the Pilot Foundation. NA.403.203

Page 143: Kiowa Cradle by Vanessa Jennings, Museum purchase with funds provided by the Pilot Foundation and Arthur Amiotte. NA.111.59

Page 144: Banner by Arthur Amiotte. NA.302.102

Page 145: Lakota High Tops. NA.202.845

Page 145: Lakota Sneakers. NA.202.846

Page 146: Chippewa-Cree Ball. NA.507.89

Page 147: Dakota Bustle. NA.203.795

Page 148: Shoshone-Bannock Vest, Debra Stone. Museum Purchase, Plains Indian Museum Aquisition Fund. NA. 202.1008

Page 149: Southern Plains Peyote Fan. NA.502.45

Page 149: Earrings by Ginger Otipoby. NA.502.53